1.00

Who Moved The Sun?

A Twin Remembers

Who Moved The Sun?
A Twin Remembers

The First Year:
What I Wanted to Ask, Tell Or Discuss With
My Twin Brother After He Passed Away.

For

Donald E. McKenzie
June 27, 1946 - September 7, 2008
My Best Friend Ever

By

Ronald A. McKenzie, Twin to Donald E. McKenzie

Published by D.E.M. Publishing,
A Division of COMPASS Consultants Corporation

Published by D.E.M. Publishing,
A Division of COMPASS Consultants Corporation

For information please contact:
COMPASS Consultants Corporation
ramckenzie.compass@gmail.com

All opinions are of the author; if I should offend anyone it was not intentional.

ISBN 978-0-578-04753-9

Printed in the United States of America

10 9 8 7 6 5 4 3 2 1

First Edition

This book is the author's reflections after his twin brother of sixty-two years passed away. The author's thoughts, comments, questions and stories are an expression of his anguish during the first year of life without his twin. It contains a lot of personal memories of what it's like to be a twin, for that is what a twinless twin is left with. It's the author's hope that these thoughts will help other twins with their secret anguish and feeling of loneliness, and help the parents and friends of twins understand the phenomenal mystery and untold joy that twins live with their whole lives.

Dedication

To DONALD E. MCKENZIE (1946-2008)

You are my hero; the best twin brother anyone could ever have. You are a part of me and part of me is gone. But I remember oh so well every minute of our life together. I am so sad, as I wanted us to spend our retirement years together helping each other when one of us needed help, as we have done all our lives. We even helped each other when we were little kids, but then, we didn't know why. It's lonely to be twinless; it also hurts deep down inside where no one can see or touch.

This book is also for:
ALL UNBORN TWINS

who are starting their life together in the warmth and comfort of their mother's womb.

OUR PARENTS

the late Janis Grace and Alonzo Max McKenzie, a wonderful loving couple who gave us the gift of life and the extra-added bonus of being identical twin brothers.

MOTHERS AND FATHERS

of all twins, born and unborn, and everyone else who want to understand the feelings that twins have.

SPOUSES AND FRIENDS OF TWINS

who have witnessed the special bond of twins and want to know how they can help their spouse or friend with the grieving process.

ALL THOSE DOCTORS AND COUNSELORS

who are faced with helping a grieving twin. This book is a starting place for understanding.

TO ALL THOSE PEOPLE

who are grieving for someone who has passed away, or those that are trying to help someone with the grieving process, and want to understand how others deal with significant and overwhelming grief and loneliness.

Like a Rolling Stone

How does it feel,
How does it feel
To be on your own
With no direction home
Like a complete unknown
Like a rolling stone ?

Single by: Bob Dylan
Writer: Bob Dylan
Producer: Tom Wilson
Song copyright© 1965; renewed 1993 by Special Rider Music
from the album Highway 61 Revisited
Released July 20, 1965

Acknowledgements

MANY PEOPLE are owed a great deal of thanks for their help and assistance to me, and I know many of them also felt the loss.

I thank Pamela, my wife for being the best wife ever and understanding what has happened to me. I also thank her for her design assistance in preparing this manuscript, and her creative labor of love in the entire text, cover & photo layout. Don would have loved the design and all the photos that are in it.

Two of Don's friends, Eleanor, and Megan Beach provided a great deal of comfort and support. They both told me stories I had not heard, and to this day Megan writes me letters that are important to me in many ways. They represent friendship and a connection to my brother that I never expected.

All of Don's friends in Eureka and Arcata, California who immediately came to my aid. David and Lou Anna Phillips took ownership of Amigo, Don's dog. David says it helps him with his grief as he was Don's best friend too. After thirty years of being apart, Don and David met twice a week for coffee to talk film after Don moved back to Arcata. Carol Davis and Patrick Conlin were there to help me work through Don's storage lockers, as was Patsy Givings, a twin herself. Carol found Don's Regional Emmy Award that I wanted so badly. I can't thank them enough.

Greg Nelson has been a good friend of both Don and I since high school. Greg and I roomed together at Cal Poly and I spent a lot of time on his family's ranch and vineyards following college. Greg was with my family when my father died; he was there when my mother passed away; and he was there with his son Tyler when Don was laid to rest on my parents' plot in California. Greg's devoted friendship and the hospitality from him and his wife, Missy, will never be forgotten.

I also want to thank a few of my co-workers: Vien-Phong Trinh (VP), and George Demarakis, at ARCON Associates, (an architectural firm in Lombard, IL.) The office was in Burnham Harbor for a summer outing, to cruise the Chicago Skyline on Lake Michigan. VP unknowingly suggested the title of this book out on the deck of a 55 ft. luxury yacht named Valara VI. As the yacht began to move, the angle of the sun changed. VP casually said: "Hey who moved the sun?" I said: "I like that, I might use it in one of my books!" George added: "Ron might not use it in his Fargo Blue Mystery novels but he could end up using it in another book!" Twenty-three days later Don passed away, and shortly afterward, I began to assemble my notes. I decided to name the book, Who Moved The Sun, for it described my feelings perfectly.

Two others deserve a special thank you. Sarah Bebee, twinless twin to Heidi, who read the manuscript and provided me with superb feedback about the overall direction of the book. I met Sarah at a Twinless Twin support group meeting and I respect her opinion and insight as a fellow twinless twin. I also want to thank Marge O'Connor who edited the manuscript. Marge has edited my work for the last fifteen years or so, and I would not be the writer I am today without all of her help.

I also want to thank Martha 'Chris' Young, Ph.D. Psychologist, who was the first person I ever talked to about the possibility of losing Don when he had his first heart attack at age thirty-six, and Dr. Mark C. Gillis, M.D. our family doctor and a father of fraternal twins who helped me in the first twenty-four hours after Don's death. And a special thanks to Dr. Christy Matusiak, D.C., who listens with her heart, and also soon to be Doctor Rob Press who introduced me to her.

Ron McKenzie, Twin to Don McKenzie

Foreword

TO ALL UNBORN TWINS: You have a wonderful life ahead of you together – you're on a journey of a lifetime that you will never forget. You're safe now cuddled together in your mother's protective womb. You are special and you will be with each other forever.

Most people don't form relationships until much later in their life; but twins start at the very beginning of their life and that's why there is so much happiness connected to the magic of being a twin. It has to be that way, so take care of each other and know that you are special. Not known to many is that identical twins are really the same age because they were conceived at the same time.

But I have some sad news for you; one of you in the future is going to experience a deep down hurt and a sense of loneliness that you can't ever begin to imagine. Every twin knows it and every twin or multiple birth child doesn't want to ever think about it.

But you must talk about it. When you're older you must sit down someday and talk about what will happen when one of you passes away. You can't do it when you're kids, but just let your emotions guide you, and when you are ready it will happen. You can start with small conversations, and then move to ones with more specifics. This book will help you do that.

This is important because it is inevitable that someday something will happen. It may be expected as in the case of a long illness, or it may be sudden. In either case, it's the most heart wrenching experience and loss you can ever experience.

One suggestion is to talk through the details between

yourselves about how the other twin will handle the loss. This may seem difficult at first, but it will comfort you both as you grow older. As you will see in the unfolding story in this book, my brother and I did talk, and we did have a plan, but now I wish our conversations had been more in depth with more detail, and that we had them even more often.

Just talking about it with your twin will help you, because even though the sun rises every day, someday for one of you it won't. That day, for me, was the worst day of my entire life. It will happen to other twins, and to other couples and friends. How we deal with it as human beings with special bonds is what this book is all about.

Carl Sagan once said "If you want to make an apple pie from scratch, you must first create the Universe." In other words, all problems go back to the beginning of time.

Creating an apple pie is relatively straightforward and doable, compared to the complexity of creating human beings – especially twins. When twins are formed they are one unit in two separate bodies that forever share the same hopes, dreams, desires, glories, frustrations, successes, and adventures. Yet, at the same time, these are different for each twin.

But what happens to this complex interaction when a twin dies? The twinless twin is left with half of all of the above. The surviving twin remains with half the hope, half the dreams, half the desires, half the glories, half the frustrations, half the successes, and half the adventures. The reason is the hopes and dreams of one twin are also the hopes and dreams of the other twin. When you become a twinless twin, you are still whole, yet half, and full of emptiness.

Who Moved The Sun?

To move forward you must use Carl Sagan's advice; you must create you own life from scratch. You must first create the Universe that is your new world. Whatever your dreams, desires, glories, frustrations, successes, and adventures are, you are creating them in your new Universe. If I close my eyes I can create my new twinless twin Universe, with my brother Don as part of it.

It's all I have, but it's enough. Barely.

Funeral Blues, by W. H. Auden (1907-1973)
Stop all the clocks, cut off the telephone,
Prevent the dog from barking with the juicy bone.
Silence the pianos and, with muffled drum,
Bring out the coffin. Let the mourners come.

Let aeroplanes circle moaning overhead,
Scribbling in the sky the message: "He is dead!"
Put crepe bows around the white necks of the public doves.
Let the traffic policemen wear black cotton gloves.

He was my north, my south, my east and west,
My working week and Sunday rest,
My noon, my midnight, my talk, my song.
I thought that love would last forever; I was wrong.

The stars are not wanted now; put out every one.
Pack up the moon and dismantle the sun.
Pour away the ocean and sweep up the wood.
For nothing now can come to any good.

# # #

Film and the visual arts have always been a very important part of our life. After college, Don left for Hollywood where he worked in the movies, produced and directed award winning documentary films, and worked at several major TV news stations. The poem Funeral Blues has been around for a long time, but I first heard it in the movie Four Weddings and a Funeral.

Table of Contents

Introduction

WHEN MY TWIN BROTHER PASSED AWAY, the world was immediately a different place, and hence the title, Who Moved The Sun? Within literally seconds after the passing of my twin brother Don, I had these thoughts. . . "I need to tell my brother this". . .or "I really need to ask Don this question and now I can't."

Since we shared everything, the list grew. At the beginning it was often an expression of my grief and the agonizing pain that hurt me so much. Other times it was just a funny sign or a slogan on a tee shirt, or a question about how to do something. No matter what, my questions, concerns, feelings and private "twin" thoughts I wanted to share with him kept coming. When they did, I would have to remind myself that I could no longer tell him something or ask a question, and my heart would sink a bit. He was gone physically from my life, and now I was alone. Even though happily married, I was really alone. My wife gave me the very best of support by understanding this devastating loneliness where half of me was gone. But still, I was alone. The worst was being in a crowded room with people – that's where I was really alone.

Thinking about it now, before he died it was as if I had this tether so that no matter where I was I was never alone. I could go to a meeting and step out for a second and call him, or text message him.

No matter where I am now, I am alone. I can no longer call my twin at noon or on the way home from work, or receive text messages from him during the day even when I'm in a meeting. Those were the most reassuring kind – those messages that pop up with some info on what Don was doing. We talked every evening while I had my glass of wine and we talked all weekend about our collaborative projects. Only a twin who has lost a twin can feel the amount of pain and loneliness that the surviving twin feels. It is an overpowering feeling of helplessness, and even with loving people around to support you, you still are standing there alone.

It's difficult for me to explain to a non-twin what it's like to be a twin. On the contrary, a twin does not know what it's like not to be a twin. I don't have a clue as to what that's like.

Being a twin is a very complex relationship; on the other hand, it's also quite simple, for you are ONE. Someone once said twins have two bodies and one soul. Some people never understand that an actual part of your life is gone; to them it's just a matter of getting back to work and enough of this melodrama. Suck it up, they say, and get on with your life. But the twin suffers a deep loss, a sadness that does not go away. It is a hole in your heart that aches continuously, and worry for the departed twin followed by feelings of survivor guilt.

The following pages represent the 365 days after Don left me. It's a measurement now; September 7th, 2008, the worst day of my life. I'm so happy that our mom and dad never had to live through this experience. I hope for a feeling of peace and happiness that Don is okay. Now I write my thoughts as they come to me. These thoughts may not perfectly match the outline of this book, but if you think about it, my life also is out of order. My thoughts come flooding to me. They are all I have.

Every day I had tons of things to share with Don, "Hey did you hear about. . ." "Did you see that. . ." "Here's an idea for a new movie. . ." "Did you ever consider . . ." "Have you tried. . ." Now, I need to share with him this way.

Who Moved The Sun?

My brother and I made an agreement we would meet at least once a year in Las Vegas, and it was not about the usual things that go on in Vegas. For us it was not constant gambling or gentlemen's clubs. We gambled a little bit, usually on our last day. We also played the ponies looking for that one winning system that we never found.

For us, Las Vegas was a place that had interesting people and where there was always something going on. There are lots of plane flights in, many spots to stay in, and endless places to eat. But this town was also the central location in our detective books called The Fargo Blue Mystery Series. On our trips, we scouted locations, ate at restaurants where Fargo and his friends would eat, and reviewed our plots and manuscripts.

One of the things that we promised each other was, when one of us passed away, the other would return to Las Vegas and experience the trip exactly the same way we had done for years. The other twin would be right there at his side, just like he is at my side this very minute. Sadly, we were just ten days away from our trip when Don passed away. Airline tickets had been bought, hotel rooms booked, suitcases readied and checklists made.

This book begins with the painful period of time when I would have been on the trip. This trip was going to be the best of the best – they all were. So, when I go, I have to make that trip the best of the best – even though Don won't be there. But he will be there; that's the complex part. The book covers my journey from that trip through September 7th, 2009, exactly one year after my tragic loss. As I began writing, I wondered how I will see the world and how much will my heart still hurt by then?

I have recorded my thoughts, questions and observations and things that I think about in several different areas as they popped into my head. But they are still somewhat chronological for the 365 days following Don's death. This is by no means a clinical book on how to deal with the loss of a twin. It is a book of my journey that chronicles my pain and how I dealt with the passing of Don. The book has deep feelings. It is meant to show other twins that what they will or have felt after the loss of their twin is similar to what all twins' experience.

Perhaps another twin, a spouse, a parent or a friend will gain a better perspective and sense of understanding as to the dynamics of this special relationship.

Having said that, I want to note that I often write as if I'm talking to Don, and refer to him in the present tense. This may be grammatically incorrect, but it underscores the difficulty that twins have: the twin that has passed is still part of the surviving twin. Their presence is always there in numerous ways that only a twin can feel. To this day I still talk of Don in the present tense. I have to.

Also, reading this book there may seem like there is a lot of repetition and redundancy. That is part of the experience; it is the constant reminder of the past that came through writing this book. If it is annoying, I apologize; but it is a direct reflection of my thought process — of memories.

Letters from Don

IN THE PROCESS OF TAKING CARE of Don's estate I found in my files a huge stack of letters that Don had sent to me over the years. Many of them were written more than twenty years ago when he was living in Venice Beach, California, working for Entertainment Tonight, and in Tokyo where he lived for over three years and worked as a news stringer, director, editor, and film maker.

These letters now have become my way of once again connecting with him, because I can read a letter that I haven't read for years, and it's like Don just wrote to me. They are included here as sound bites, as they say in his profession, that bring back so many memories; and memories are what this book is all about — they are what remain.

Ron, Twin to Don

Letters from Don
On Coffee

"Remember the coffee we used to have in the morning in Hong Kong? Also the meals at the Regent Hotel by the water, or at The Peninsula Hotel. They are a good place to have coffee, breakfast, and read the China Morning Post."

One
My First Thoughts

IT'S NOT FAIR. I hurt so bad. There is so much more we could have done together. We were planning the rest of our lives, and now it's over.

The realization I will never receive another phone call, or an email or a text message devastates me to the point I can barely process the information.

We talked everyday, constantly. Oh my, what are we going to do? How are we going to communicate? I am lost without you.

I feel so alone now and yet I feel you are near and at the same time, part of me is gone.

This worries me a lot. If I had died and you had lived, you would be out there in Eureka all by yourself, living by yourself. Knowing now what I know as to the tremendous hurt and loss, you would have had a really bad time as you would have few people to talk to. It would have been a living nightmare. I have Pamela and she is tremendous support, but you would have had no one close, and you would have really been alone. Pamela said that she is my better half and you were my other half. You didn't have that and I worried about it.

Don, I will keep our Las Vegas experience alive; I will go there at least once a year and stay at The Orleans Casino and do all of the things that we do. I know for a fact that you will be with me and we will be together. I will find new secrets out there for us, and I know you will be there to share them.

I feel like you're on a big trip someplace with no phones. But that's okay; we will talk when you get back.

Is being in Heaven like being on vacation?

Can you see me?

Good News! David and Lou Anna have adopted your Dog Amigo, and he now lives in the Redwoods. Or to say it more accurately, Amigo adopted them. I got a call from David – Amigo saw and chased his first deer. David said Amigo spent the following day sleeping.

There should be a twin law that says the twin in heaven gives a call after about a week to say everything is fine – enjoy your life and be happy for I am with you, and someday we will be together again. The real secret is that every twin knows that this law already exists and works just fine.

I have this strange feeling you are with me.

Don, you are my hero.

Remember just a couple of days before you died we were saying . . . be happy because we have our health and that's what's really important.

Do you cry when I cry?

Part of my loss is I always knew you were there. For the last twelve years when you owned your bookstores I could always call, and you always would be there. Don, you were always there for me. Now, my phone is painfully silent, and it is a constant reminder of how much I miss you.

Every time my phone rings I think it's you calling me and then I remember it won't be. It's someone else, and I'm again reminded of my loss and I sink a bit lower.

I know that you were very proud that I am an architect. I also know you knew in college how often I had no money for food but somehow I managed. Like we will now.

Don, now I know why you loved the Pacific Northwest in Arcata, California. When I landed in Chicago after spending 10 days out there, the air smelled funny, not like the fresh ocean air or the view of the tall redwood trees or the vineyards where you are buried.

I woke up this morning and figured I would give you a call at about 10:30 am right after I got my haircut. Then I realized I couldn't call you any more.

How in the hell do you open your email?

I'm packing up your place. You have five wallets. Why do you have five wallets with stuff in them?

I am no longer afraid of dying.

Don, now you won't be able to see my health club that I go to, or my new Palm Phone that I was so excited about.

I remembered on the first weekend home after I got back from packing up your place, that on Sunday, the day you left me, we were talking on the phone and I said I was outside barbequing and having a glass of wine, and that it was a perfect evening and had been a perfect day. We were talking about our projects and your acid reflux and I remember starting to feel concerned because you kept talking about it. About four hours later you died. I guess sometimes when you think it's a perfect day, it really may not be, but you just don't know it yet. As it turned out, it was the worst day of our lives.

I feel guilty that I wasn't there to help you and that I didn't take care of you better.

As you drove yourself to the emergency room and we talked on the phone I was beginning to get scared; I knew someday this would happen but I didn't want it to happen. You said the symptoms were different from your first heart attack, so I thought about it differently.

When you texted me and said, "call for a sec" I did, and then I knew something was wrong when you said "I'm really scared." I could hear it in your voice. Then I was scared. Oh, so scared and I convinced you to go to the hospital and I talked to you on the way. General stuff. Your last words to me were, "I just want to get past this and get to Vegas."

I wanted us to grow old together; to be able to sit back and reflect on the things we have done and seen; and talk about our writing projects. It's all I ever wanted.

Don, I picture you driving to the hospital and I feel guilty I wasn't there to help. I worry about how scared you were. What were you thinking about? Oh I want to know so badly.

I know when they took you in, you immediately started to have problems breathing; then they said you passed out. Oh Don, I hope you didn't suffer. I hope your thoughts were of the wonderful life we had as twins. I am so scared right now; I have so much grief that it hurts me. But as we had said, we must be strong. But it's hard right now as I feel you have been cheated. I must rebuild my life, but it's difficult because you're not here. But I will rebuild it; with you at my side, everyday, every waking minute.

Don, do I dream of new dreams, or do I dream of our dreams? I can't dream of new dreams because our dreams are all that matter to me. In **Noble House**, by James Clavell he uses the term "Joss" which means fate: good or bad.

As we both understand, Joss.

Letters from Don
On Food

"I miss our meals at the Chart House in Malibu on the Pacific Coast Highway. It would be nice to go there and to have a few drinks by the ocean and have a good meal."

Letters from Don
On Work

"I think Nancy and I will be interviewing three top executives from NBC, ABC and CBS regarding movies of the week for TV Guide. I am also preparing for an interview with Michael Douglas of **Streets of San Francisco** which I will do when they are back in production. My work as a location scout for the show in San Francisco is going to pay off."

Two
My Emotions Take Over

I WONDER IF I'LL EVER PLAY GOLF AGAIN.

One twin goes to heaven and the other twin is left in a living hell of loneliness.

Oh, Don, I miss you so much. I cried at lunch today. That's when I would talk to you. I cried really hard as I miss you so much and I don't know what's going to come along in my life to ever replace my feelings. Of course, the answer is nothing can ever replace you. I have lost something so big in my life I feel hopelessly lost.

Ever since we were small we have shared all of our experiences. From the days when we were learning to do magic, to when we drove across the United States with mom after dad died even though we only had learners' permits; from spending time swimming in Wisconsin at Lake Neshonoc with Linda and Julie Anderson, to our days in high school, our first jobs and our first days of college, we shared everything. Now, who do I share with?

It doesn't seem fair that you have been taken from me. I am without a course; I have no horizon; my tears cloud my vision of the future; and I have no plan. Where am I to go?

God, can you heal me of my pain?

Now I feel I do things alone. If I have a lunch meeting I'm thinking I can catch you before the meeting and then we can talk after the meeting. Then I realize I can't do that and it seems like I am out there without protection.

I'm lost without you. Even things when I do the things I did alone before, I now feel somewhat abandoned because I always felt you were there. Yet, in a way, it is the same now. I feel you are there, and that is so comforting. I just can't talk to you.

I lost the only person I played games with such as chess, GO, bridge and Playstation. I lost my twin, but what I really lost was your understanding and complete acceptance. It's hard to have half a soul; that's the major adjustment that twinless twins must make.

I found out that when one of us bought something, we would often purchase two of them, like two Mason coffee cups, or two money clips, or two Fargo Blue polo shirts. That was a twin thing. And when we bought something individually, the other would unknowingly buy the same thing. I bought two identical Urns so ours would be the same; I was in so much pain I was trying to do everything right for you. I have thirty some boxes in my basement and when I unpack a lot of your things it turned out I already have the same items. What one had, the other one had.

I'm reading an old note from you. What does the word "nxcrdsf" mean? I can never decipher your handwriting. I found your accounts and passwords. But let me be the first one to tell you that ******* does not help me figure out your password.

Don, I so much miss working on our dreams together.

I have been thinking about how our lives paralleled and how they were different. I was always worried about you and concerned that you seemed to have less, yet when we were together, you were happy. You showed me that the key to life is happiness from within.

You were more of an artist than I ever was.

Don, Today I saw my shadow and it looks just like you.

Letters from Don
On handicapping the ponies

"I am anxious to play the ponies again. I actually had five winners for the day, but handicapping on paper is different from being at the track. I hope you got my note to play $2 Win and $4 Place instead of playing Across-the-Board. I got lucky as the second place money horses were winning all the races."

Letters from Don
On The Playboy Club

"I went to a Playboy Club here in L.A. and had a drink served to me by a Bunny. She didn't want to start a long lasting relationship, or a short one for that matter. Of course, there is always Donna, the former Playboy Bunny that I introduced you to that cuts our hair."

Three
The Las Vegas Trip That We Missed
SEPTEMBER 30, 2008

THIS IS THE LAST DAY before we were to go on our trip. Who would ever think that we would not make this trip together? Not once did we ever postpone our trips — not once. And now, I can't go. I loved leaving the office on this day as I knew within twenty-four hours I would see you.

Today, I had to drive about fifty miles and I left in the morning. It's fall and the trees are showing spectacular colors. The air was crisp. As soon as I started to drive I had this feeling that part of me was not there. It was on my left side. But I also had this feeling that something was there. It was about the size of me and it was next to me. I also felt that I was alone, but the sensation next to me comforted me greatly.

Before, the sensation had always been in front and to the right of me. Now, it moved over to the side you are always on, which is on my left. As we had discussed, we only felt comfortable when you were on my left, and we think we were in the womb that way. I feel better and comforted but I also feel this huge sense of being alone and part of me is gone.

For the next seven days I will live the trip in my mind. As we promised each other, I will go back and do the trip exactly how we would do it. It's what is holding me together right now. It is the only way I can be someplace and know you are right there next to me.

17

I think about our trips to Las Vegas a lot. It wasn't all the glitz and glamour, although that added to the trip. It was really all about seeing each for the first time; doing a high five that we made it, being there together again; waking up in the morning and deciding what we felt like doing that day and us never having a problem agreeing. If one of us wanted something, then we would do it and the other twin would be happy because we were doing something that the other one really wanted to do.

We have spots in Las Vegas where we like to be. The only ones who know those spots are you and I. When I pass away someday, those spots will disappear. In my mind I am going to those spots; I can visualize them and they are there waiting for us to see or touch. It's so unfair to me that you are gone, Don. I miss you so much.

Today is the first day of our trip to Las Vegas and it is the first trip we have missed together. It is such a different day. I would have seen you today – you would have been standing by the rail where you always stood, and your hand would shoot up in the air when you saw me coming, and we would be ONE again. It's a sad day; I cried several times at work.

On this trip to Las Vegas that we missed I pass the milestone of one month since you are gone. Oh my, what great plans we had and look what happened. Instead you are gone and we are left without that trip. How many times did we talk about how many trips we had left before we couldn't travel anymore?

Let's see, over the next ten years if we saw each other two times a year, then that would only be twenty times we would be together, and then we would be seventy-two years old. So each trip is important and in fact we decided to try to make it three times a year. And now, it's over. Thankfully we did make those trips together for the last fifteen years. It's those memories that now keep me going. But what really keeps me going for the long haul is knowing I will be with you one day, and we'll have new adventures together.

I went to Starbucks today for some peace. I just wanted to be alone in a crowd, and I was.

Driving home at night is the worst. That is when I always called you. That's when I cry. I save up all day, and then I cry.

Most people raise their eyebrows when I tell them we meet in Las Vegas. They think, ahaaaa, they must hit all the topless bars and stuff. But we never did that – it was too much fun being together. So let other people have their imaginations and we will have ours.

Where are your passwords?

I have been reading your email as a way to find people and to try to get your estate in order. Apparently you got the consulting assignment you were after. That makes me happy. You also got another call you had been waiting for on another consulting assignment. Everything was going your way.

I was looking forward to when we retired and we could play golf and bet two dollars at the track and have a great time—we just had to be together to have a great time. Now I will do it alone—with you.

I just remembered that one of our dreams was to have an office in that building on Sahara where Fargo Blue has his office. It would be a place for us to go to work on our writing and our projects. Now when I see that I will think of all the times we walked around it dreaming, thinking, and talking.

Eleanor is your friend in Oregon that you loved to talk with. She returned my phone call and we talked for quite a while. Don, she is brilliant and I can see why she was special in your life. The stories she told of things that happened to her forty or fifty years ago were incredible. I told her I was going to call her from time-to-time, and asked her to call me whenever she wanted to. I also promised that when I'm in Oregon I will visit her. She made me feel better.

Eleanor said that I should think of you now as if you were on a long visit to a Tibetan Monastery high in the mountains doing research. You are not able to receive mail or phone calls, but your thoughts can come to me. Eleanor was a great comfort to me.

I'm still looking for your passwords.

Don, I'm okay even if I'm crying.

Sometimes I look in the mirror and I see you. Or I will be talking to Pamela and feel like I sound just like you.

One of the things I will miss is going into the elevators in Vegas and having someone ask "Are you twins?" We always liked that. And then I always asked which one is heavier? And everyone would laugh.

Remember when we were growing up in Willits, California we would get large cardboard boxes from the garbage behind Dad's store, and haul them out on the hill behind our house, and then slide down the hill with that tall oat grass flying in our face. And we built a track of sorts and would have races that always ended in crashes. NASCAR was born there and we were in about the fifth and sixth grade. I remember these things now and wish I could talk with you and remember them together.

Who Moved The Sun?

Don, I found a whole box full of X-File cards and remembered how we played that game at the Monte Carlo Casino Food Court.

I was at work and glanced at the time and found myself daydreaming about when we were kids playing in Willits, climbing rocks and trees. We used to climb those two boulders and sit there and talk for hours. We walked to school everyday rain or shine. I looked back at the clock on my desk and one minute had gone by.

I'm at a seminar and as the speaker speaks I'm thinking about how much I miss you. We always liked taking seminars together. I know we had some goals to take some seminars in Las Vegas. I will try to attend one so that I can continue to do the things we would have done together.

I think often about how that day neither one of us had a clue what was going to happen. I mean, even when you were driving to the hospital and I was talking to you, I was not thinking that this was a life or death situation. And I know you were scared, but I don't think you thought it would be fatal either. If you had made it I would have done whatever was necessary to get you back on track and living in your place so we could visit Las Vegas. And I know you would have worked hard to make that happen. But that is all gone now, and I'm struck by the suddenness of it -- such finality on an average day where we talked numerous times and laughed and made plans for our upcoming trip.

There could have been a million possible scenarios and when I think of the "What if's" I go crazy.

The hardest part of every day is each minute. The really hard part is leaving work at the end of the day, because I know I can't call you up on the phone as I have done almost forever.

Don, you have a job to do. A project if you will. You must help me in my life by guiding me and protecting me. I need your counsel daily. I know that you will be there to listen to me and to help me and are there waiting for me.

As we both know, someday I will join you. And when that happens, we will toast each other, and we both know what that toast will be, for it is the only one-word toast that explains everything in a way that makes living bearable: Joss. It is what it is.

My biggest fear is that I will not find anything in my future that excites me as much as when I knew you and I were going to get together and do our "twin" brother thing. I worry about this.

I was at the Kane County Flea Market today and you did not call.

Remember when we used to go outside at night, you in Oregon and me in Illinois, and we would look at the Moon at the same time. That was our way of being together. No one knew about that one.

Can you see the constellations from where you are?

Today I have intense back pain to the point I could not go to work. Lifting all of those boxes finally caught up with me. But I'm glad for the pain because I was able to help you.

I wonder if you can watch movies up there?

Letters from Don
On Acting

"I'm getting 25,000 yen for an acting role I did.
It was an honor to be directed by Ichikawa Kon in his
film Rockmegan at Toho Studios. So, I'm living in Japan
and now I'm an actor."

Letters from Don
On Money

"Money is still a problem. I've got a photo essay in
Hong Kong to shoot. I think it's from the article you sent
to me on the snake store – the guy blowing up the snakes.
I have enough information to write a short article for
Newlook Magazine to accompany the photo essay.
What a way to make a living."

Letters from Don
On Experience

"Since leaving Humboldt Theater Arts Department in 1973
I have worked as a film and video editor in newsrooms in
San Francisco where I cut the Patty Hearst kidnapping story
that ended up as a national feed to the networks, edited for
Los Angeles news stations, freelanced on several motion picture
productions, entered the mainstream of Hollywood and
worked for George Slaughter Productions on Real People and
Speak Up America, and then spent five years
at Entertainment Tonight as a video tape editor and field
producer. I worked in various production capacities in Tokyo,
Japan and Hong Kong including a project at Shaw Studios
where the Bruce Lee films were done."

Letters from Don
In Hong Kong

"It's after my evening meeting and I had a great time.
I spent most of it talking with Victoria Hearst, sister
of Patty Hearst. She's an actress specializing in karate and
is up for a part in a Cannon film. She learned about my
project in Hong Kong, and she gave me her photographs
on the spot. She met Sir Run Run Shaw twice."

Four
Getting By Day-By-Day

I WAS THINKING ABOUT HAVING WORRIES.

When did we not have them? I thought about our time in Willits. I can't remember worrying about anything significant when we were there. We had our school, our acreage to explore, and the small creeks to run and play in. We had big rocks to climb and tons of poison oak that gave us a rash, almost on a regular basis. We had Saturday afternoon movies that cost twenty-five cents; ten cents to get in and ten cents for the coke and five cents for the popcorn. The movie also had a bonus weekly adventure serial. That's what all the kids talked about during the week. Do you remember the one with the boulder being rolled down the hill to wipe out the shack where the pretty girl was hiding?

Should I continue to read and study French? We spent a lot of time studying different languages including French and Japanese.

Remember the Noya Theater in Willits? And the Saturday dad wanted us to help him with a new lumber supply store where he had invested in as a partner? We worked that Saturday, even though it was the weekend a big movie was playing that all the kids were talking about. We were sick about not being able to go, and we complained, but we still had to help dad. Do you remember that? Talking about memories like this is one thing that twins miss, for the other twin remembers different parts and it's always a surprise. It's usually followed by "I forgot about that." I will miss those conversations.

If you watch movies in heaven, are the endings different? If Pam and I are watching a movie, are you watching it with us?

I haven't received a letter from you lately.

I called Alan Gianoli to tell him about you. He was devastated. Ahaaaa. . . you could have left a little bit more money in your checking account.

Now I know how Robert and Ted Kennedy felt when Jack Kennedy was taken away, and how Ted felt when Robert was taken away.

I wonder if we would have stayed together longer if we lived in the same area; if it would have made a difference. I think about that a lot.

OCTOBER 21, 2008

Today is 44 days since I heard your voice, your laugh, your worries, your concerns, your happiness. But most of all, it's 44 days since I felt like I was a whole person. I'm here alone, yet I feel you next to me; but just the same, it hurts to be so alone. Don, I still cry everyday, but I know you want me to be happy and to enjoy life. I am getting there but still have a long way to go.

It is also 216 days since I shared coffee with you the morning of March 19th, 2008, had breakfast at The Orleans, walked around the hotel together, stood by the alligators and gave them a pat, traveled to the airport and then out to the gates, and then one last hug and handshake before I left. You had to go through security at a different gate than me. I walked down the long corridor, and turned, and I gave you one last wave, and you were looking for it and your hand shot up and returned the wave. That was the last time I saw you. But we knew we would be back.

As it turned out, no one knew that was our last good bye. But at least it was done well, and it will last a lifetime. It has to. As Clint Eastwood said in Absolute Power, "Tomorrow is a promise to no one."

I was so proud that you broke into Hollywood, worked there and shared that experience with me. Leonard Maltin wrote me a note today and said he really liked working with you. I am so proud of you.

You probably met more people from different parts of the world than most. Think of the people you met and worked with in Japan. How about Saho who helped you learn Japanese, or the two Japanese girls you introduced me to, or the other Japanese girl who took us to the Teriyaki Grill in Japan.

I now realize that part of being together in Las Vegas that we liked, but never spoke of, is we could take care of each other. Approximately fourteen days a year we could make sure the other one was all right.

Each night in Las Vegas, I was happy that you were there and everything was okay. I didn't have to call you or text you or to wait for a call in the morning. You were right there.

What books are you reading now?

Do you remember in Willits lying on top of the hill in back of our house way beyond the big rock down by the stream? We would lie on our backs and watch the clouds billow across the skies. We laid there and talked about things. Those were the best of times. We were only about nine or ten years old.

Do you remember as kids riding in the car from Willits to Ukiah, California and we used to look down at the ranch and see the racetrack? No one knew then who the racehorse was that used to live there. When the movie Seabiscuit came out it mentioned that Ridgewood Ranch was where Seabiscuit went to rest and get well, and where they buried him, under an unmarked oak tree.

Our dad died in the hospital that Charles S. Howard, the owner of Seabiscuit, donated money to build after he lost his son, Frank R. Howard. How could we ever imagine that dad's J.C. Penney store sign would be next to the Seabiscuit display in the Mendocino County museum? We discovered that at the same time. Wow, that was really something.

I also just found out about another possible tie to Seabiscuit. It's very likely that the Harry Casey Best painting that dad and mom bought at Bargain Lane in Redwood Valley came from the estate of Charles S. Howard. The store is on Highway 101, almost across the road from the entrance to Ridgewood Ranch. Howard died in 1950 and our parents bought the painting in about 1956, when Howard's estate was liquidated.

I just received a special invitation to attend a ceremony at the Ridgewood Ranch for the unveiling of Seabiscuit's U.S. Postage stamp. I'm not attending, but it makes me or us connected once again to the famous horse that we sort of grew up with.

Movies were always part of our lives and we both loved the one about Seabiscuit. It brought back memories of when we were kids. Another movie we both liked was Dreamer. It was a story about a horse and a little girl played by Dakota Fanning who had total belief in her horse Soñador. She taught her father what real belief was all about. From that movie came these inspirational words read by Cale Crane (Dakota Fanning) to her horse Soñador, which in Spanish means "Dreamer." When I read them now, I think of you.

The Way to Victory
You are a great champion.
When you ran,
The ground shook,
The sky opened,
And mere mortals parted.
Parted the way to victory,
Where you'll meet me in the winner's circle,
Where I'll put a blanket of flowers on your back.

The movie was inspired by a true story and directed and written by John Gains.© DreamWorks Pictures, Gatins, John, et. al. Final shooting script, 09-13-04, p. 103; IMDB

Don, someday I will meet you in the winners' circle.

We used to say "We always have Las Vegas." We created that from the line in the movie Casablanca that was "We'll always have Paris." As you said in one of your notes, ". . .and we have Las Vegas, which is so important." To us that meant that when we were there, everything was perfect, everything was in order and as twin brothers we were free to explore anything we wanted. It had everything to do with being together from dawn to dusk and falling asleep in the same room, just like we did when we were little kids. Everything was right with the world. From the first sip of coffee to the last sip of wine.

It had nothing to do with gambling or the nightclubs. It seemed that when we were in Las Vegas we had no worries. Of course we did, but we talked about them and then put them in a little box as we learned to do from reading Noble House. The key was we were together.

I remember we used to have a conversation about two or three subjects at the same time with out breaking the rhythm. It happens to a lot of people, but in a different and more complicated way with twins. Some say it's a twin thing. Don, of course you know, the problem I'm faced with is that when I go to Las Vegas next time, you won't be meeting me there. But, as we discussed, you will be right there next to me.

Don, I went to my Wheaton Masonic Lodge 269 tonight. It was difficult for me to walk in and to talk to everyone. I took my seat as Treasurer, and the meeting seemed to open and close quickly. Sitting there my heart was not in it as much as it was in the past. I was very happy however, that together we accomplished our goals of becoming Master Masons, the highest you can go in Freemasonry. If I was trying to do that now, I don't know if I could complete it. Yet, I know you would have wanted me to.

At the end of the evening, someone asked for a moment of silence for another Lodge member that had passed away. Then I stood up, and with a broken voice asked for the same for you. All the members stood up, and there was a long silence of bowed heads in your memory. I was crying.

I can remember the day we decided to become Freemasons together. It was in Las Vegas. We were in our hotel having a glass of wine when we discussed it and decided to do it. When we got home we started checking it out, and a day or so later you called and said, "I'm in!" Of course, that meant you had made contact with a lodge member. And the message to me was "you better get started if we're going to do this together." Of course, I did. We did it together even though we were in separate states. I'm so happy for that and having the shared memory.

I am working at putting my life's affairs in perfect order so I can spend more free time thinking about our life and time together. Does that make any sense?

NOVEMBER 7, 2008

It's been two months now since you passed away. I have a feeling of despair, of hopelessness, that I will never be totally happy again. Deep down inside of me I am filled with anguish about the future. I am in a phase where I am existing but with great sadness in my heart. I still worry about you; but you are in a much better place. I pray to God you are happy. Your job is to guide me; to be my protector, to be the brother that you always were.

Don, it seems that everything I do reminds me of you. And then I realized, that everything I did, no matter what, was connected to you. I was walking down the aisle of a grocery store and I walked past the assortment of hot sauces and saw the one you showed me in Las Vegas. I am glad that everything reminds me of you as that means I am going to be thinking of you forever. That to me is perfect. Lonely, but perfect.

One of the things that always amazed me was how you would bring up something about growing up that I had completely forgotten about. Or I would say something and you would tell me that you had forgotten it. Now, I must rely on my own memory.

Today I took 355 South to visit a school district. As I was driving I suddenly noticed a Bass Pro Shop off to the right. I knew it was there, but today it reminded me of the Saturday I had been there and called you as I went up and down the aisles. I realized that I could never do that again. Everything reminds of me of you.

Don, I was sorting out your fishing equipment and I realized that you never caught a fish. Not one fish after about three years. How embarrassing. I mean, you did, a long time ago when we were kids. But when you decided to start fishing in Oregon I was all for it. You bought your stuff and we talked about it, and then fly fishing. Then you started to look at it and bought a fly outfit in Las Vegas. Then around the time of your separation, your ex-wife started to cause you unbelievable problems encompassing both your business and your relationship with her. It literally destroyed you. Suddenly, for you, there was no pleasure in fly fishing anymore.

I remember your last fishing trip. You were worried about the situation and then it all came apart, and it was none of your doing. When it was all over, you moved back to California and the fishing dream started to come back. You began checking out the rivers. We bought some DVD's and watched them together in Las Vegas. And, then you went over to the other side. So, I'm going to put a note on one of your pictures "Gone Fishing."

Don, I just figured out one of the problems I'm facing. I no longer have a rainbow to look forward to. For the last fifteen years or so, we always had a Las Vegas trip in the works. We pretty much knew when we left Vegas when we'd be back. So even on the hardest days when things didn't go well, I always had the pleasant thought in the back of my mind that Las Vegas was right around the corner. It was something to look forward to, as we would be together again. I know you felt the same way, and that is why you wanted that March trip the year after you moved away from the troubles you had to deal with. And I also know you wanted that September trip so badly in 2008. I know part of it was to give you a rest from all the challenges you were facing. We were going to the end of the rainbow and we didn't even know it. Now, I have no more rainbows to look for with you.

Remember how we developed the Fargo Blue Mystery Series so we could eventually become known as Las Vegas authors? The plan was that casinos would comp us to stay at their hotel and we would do book signings. Well, we made it into Las Vegas Life Magazine, but now we won't be sharing that dream. At least we had a plan. It's more than many brothers have.

We lived our separate lives but we always shared. Anything I had was yours if you wanted it. We will always be twins and I will still share everything I have with you.

Unfortunately, the best departure for twins is when they die together at the same time. Then the knife-like inner pain would not exist in the survivor.

Letters from Don
On Bruce Lee

"We got to the front gate of Shaw Studios on the backside of Hong Kong. It was sort of like an army guard shack. We eventually met with Jenny Li. I showed her the photographs from the Paramount Studios lot with both you and I in it as we looked over the studio sets. We never mentioned we needed financing. I left for a couple of minutes and Richard conveyed that McKenzie had worked in production for five years for Entertainment Tonight. He showed her a letter from Paramount, and when I got back Jenny Li arranged for a tour of the back lot where the Bruce Lee films were done. We looked at the different areas that would fit Vampire High, including streets that looked like San Francisco over by the park by the Golden Gate Bridge."

"On the way back we spotted sixteen Rolls Royce's and Richard asked who they were owned by. It turns out that they were owned by Sir Shaw who had been knighted by the Queen. We went back and photographed all the areas so we could start to develop our story boards."

Five
The Holidays

THE HOLIDAYS HAVE STARTED. Halloween is here and I always enjoyed the glorious colors of the leaves as they start to turn. But now, this year, I find no enjoyment at all in thoughts of the upcoming holiday season and a new year. My life is so much different now; I have lost the drive, the enthusiasm for day-to-day activities. My reward was always sharing these with you, and now I am in this large abyss where nothing excites me.

I think about our Halloween experiences. When we were in Ukiah, California, we were really bad with all of those water balloon fights with the other neighborhood kids. Don't tell anyone.

I also remember a long time ago, in Boise, Idaho when we were really small, probably second or third grade. It was fall just before Halloween. We were over at friends of mom and dad's, Paul and Betty Swanson, who were from the J.C. Penney Store where dad worked after getting out of the TB hospital. There were leaves everywhere so we buried you in a gigantic pile of leaves. Then we called Paul over and pretended we lost you. Of course he knew you were under there, but it was the fun of it all. I think of that now that I just buried you. For real. You are now under a pile of leaves forever, and it has changed my life.

Do you remember being in Las Vegas during Halloween? Wow, that was something. Let's go again.

Thanksgiving turned out different this year. At the last minute Pam and her sister had to be with her mom, who had a series of medical appointments and needed Pam's help. I agreed that it was the right decision for her to go. It reminded me of one of the things we talked about as our mom was getting older was how we wished we would have spent more time with her in her last days, particularly when she lived in California. Every minute with a loved one is a precious minute you will never get back.

So, this Thanksgiving I cooked a complete turkey dinner for myself and watched a movie. I would have talked to you throughout the day, and of course I missed that. But it gave me a chance to try out my wings at being alone. I cried. I tried to share the day with you as much as I could.

I still keep the phone next to me when Pam and I watch movies. I enjoyed oh so much the buzzing that signaled a text message from you. That gave me so much pleasure and happiness. Then at a break in the movies, I would glance at it, and would text you back. That is what I miss in my life right now. No one can ever replace that. That's why it's so tough.

One of my all time favorite times was going out and buying you something for Christmas, wrapping it and getting it in the mail so you had something to open at Christmas. But Pamela and I wanted you to have something. I know you never received a Christmas present in almost twenty years in your personal relationship with your spouse and that always made me sad. Not even from your in-laws even though you spent time and money to be there, and bought them all presents. Of course it's not fair, or right. It's only a reflection of how they were raised. So what do I do this year?

The hell with it. I'm buying you a present anyway. I just have to figure out how to ship it.

Who Moved The Sun?

We always talked a lot on the holidays. The conversations were always good. What I now realize is that I miss thinking about what you're thinking about. I miss worrying about what you're worrying about. I miss your happiness, and I miss your sadness, because then I could help you.

Now, I don't have your current thoughts in my head about what's happening; what you are worried about; how your day went, the wine you had last night, and the countless other things that surround you. Now I realize, it also made up my day. Maybe that's the hole that is inside of me; the missing piece that all twins feel. Aha, it is; I miss what you're thinking and feeling.

Now it's the Christmas season and time to be merry. The biggest struggle I have is being happy. It doesn't seem like Christmas without you in my life. I see other people and they are genuinely excited about the season and shopping. But to me, it is a sullen reminder of how difficult it really is to be a twinless twin.

Remember when we used to go with mom to Union Square in San Francisco, and we always looked at the Macy's windows and then had a treat in the inside where they had an ice cream parlor. Don, I hope you can see those windows.

I also remember taking mom to Union Square the last time. I had to almost hold her up; it was cold and crowded but we made it all the way around the block to see the Christmas decorations in the store windows. I knew that would be the last time she saw those windows and I think she also knew it. But it was also the last time I saw those windows at Christmas time. I would like to see them again but it would be difficult to be there at Christmas. Maybe you and I will see them together in the future. I hope so. Nothing better at Christmas time than Union Square and a walk down Maiden Lane.

We probably saw these stores several times together as we used to meet at that corner restaurant after you got off of work at KGO. That's where Bebe the waitress worked. She liked us because we were twins. Union square was like home to us.

This Christmas I don't have the same spirit as before. I'm working hard to remember that I must be happy. I can still be happy and enjoy things even if you have passed away. It hurts me so much. I'll be doing something, and then all of a sudden I remember that you are not there.

Most people can't understand how terrible it is to experience the death of your twin. I read stories on the Twinless Twin site and feel badly that so many people hurt as much as I do. It's so hard, Don. But I am trying to do things and be happy for us. I know that's what you would want.

The biggest problem that a twinless twin has is a deep, indescribable loneliness. It's there no matter what is going on. It's worse during the holidays as memories come flooding back about all the great times we had together. Even if we were separated by distance, knowing that the other twin was okay was all it took for us to have a good Christmas. Now, the void is there, but the memories continue, and I live in those memories.

Christmas morning has come and gone. Pam and I opened our presents. I bought you two presents and one from you to me. So I opened them and I cried. But it was a way for me to spend Christmas with you.

Later someone told me that when I bought those presents and opened them and cried that I was being negative. Can you imagine that? Many people have no clue as to what I'm going through.

That is something that many other twinless twins experience —
the lack of understanding by other people of the special and
unbreakable bond between twins that remains when one of them
departs.

New Year's Eve has come and gone, and with it are the feelings
about a lost brother whom I will never see again, talk with, hang out
in Vegas with, write with, drink wine with, watch movies with and a
hundred other things that seem small, but are oh so important now
that I can't do them. New Years is gone and so are you. Oh how I
miss you.

Letters from Don
On Writing

"I still have an idea to write a short novel – fiction –
about a average American family – two kids – five and
six – girl and boy – station wagon – two car garage -
vacations – the supermarket – church – a backyard
with a swing – swimming lessons in the summer –
snow in the winter – a fireplace – neighborhood fights –
business meetings – teas – color television – and a bird
in a birdcage – all told through the eyes of a cat and her kittens."

Six
Alone In Las Vegas

I MADE THE RESERVATIONS this morning. In the middle of deciding which flight and all the other details I started to cry. I'm excited about the trip, but I also know that you will not be at our meeting place when I get there. I will look for you, but you will not be there, or maybe you will be there. I will still wave to you like I always have. No one around me will know what is going on. No one around me will know or understand the pain I will be in. No one around me will care.

Picture a crowded Las Vegas airport with people arriving and happy to be there; amongst them is a stranger holding a Starbucks cup of coffee and dragging a tote bag on wheels. That will be me and no one will know of the tremendous hurt inside of me.

But I will know. I am learning that I can go through life sad and miserable, or I can go through life with all the wonderful memories of when we were together. Life is full of "stuff" and life is what you make of it. I know now that I will be sad at times on this trip, but I will also be happy because I know you are going to be right there next to me. There are only two feelings in life: fear and joy. Joy is hard for me right now, but it is the right road to take. Joy will allow me to experience life with you at my side.

So, I have the flight, hotel and car rentals all made. I can hardly wait to get there. Watch for me. I'll wave when I see the spot where you usually stand, waiting.

* * *

41

I'm in Las Vegas now. You weren't there, standing, waiting for me. But I knew and felt your presence.

I was excited, but knew in the back of my mind I was in for disappointment. That would be walking up to the spot where you always stood and you wouldn't be there. The hurt of it all is going to overwhelm me. I can see you so clearly. Your hand would shoot up and we knew the world was once again a perfect place. This is the trip that I will learn that the world is not a perfect place and that we have little control over our destinies. It will hurt me a great deal to walk up to that rail. I plan to stay there for a bit savoring the moment; remembering all the times of happiness. I will do my best to be all right.

I cried on the phone when I called Pam from the airport. I also cried when I got to the hotel room. After that, I started to be okay.

You are everywhere. There is not a place I go that I do not feel your presence. We did so many things here, everywhere I turn there is a memory.

I'm remembering a lot of things about our times in Las Vegas. This trip is bringing them all back. Everything I see I think of things; where we played pool; where we played catch in the park like we did when we were kids; where we went to the movies by the MGM Grand; the trip to Area 51; the Wizard of Oz, Emerald City and gigantic Lion entrance to MGM, and the location of our first mystery novel; the first time we saw Fry's on our way to see the movie Seabiscuit; staying at the Sahara after so many years; watching New York, New York, the Bellagio and the other casinos being built; winning a jackpot on the slot machine on the last trip; going out for coffee together in the morning and glad to do it; playing Texas Hold'em at the Excalibur, and many others. Your favorite was stepping outside to see the Orleans sign light up. So many memories; it makes me happy and it makes me sad. It makes me pray and it makes me cry. It makes me miss you more and more as each minute of my life ticks away.

I remember you so well and how happy we were together in Vegas. You were beaming and happy. I also knew and could sense you had a lot of deep down worry and that bothered me too. I can remember being saddened sometimes when we compared things about our lives and you had to do without some things or could not afford the best. This hurt me, but I didn't always tell you. It felt as if my life was easier in some ways; but really it wasn't, just different. We agreed we each have our trials and I couldn't live your life, and you couldn't live mine. But we had our own life together as twins.

As for material things, we knew it didn't matter a bit once we were together. We were one; and the only part that hurt was having to say goodbye.

After our very first trip it was one year between that goodbye and the next time we saw each other. During that year we wrote letters back and forth and talked about nothing else but the next trip. We each read the same handicapping books. We could hardly wait to go. As the trip got nearer we worked even harder at making everything perfect.

Each time we got to Vegas, when we saw each other we were instantly happy, and the world was a better place. We knew it was the beginning of another wonderful time together as twin brothers.

Sometimes I'll go into a dark room, close my eyes, and visualize myself walking up the ramp toward the area where you would be waiting at the Las Vegas McCarran Airport. I walk past the Starbucks and the bookstore and the Lindo Michoacán Mexican Restaurant, on Desert Inn, and then I can see you standing there. I wave and you wave back. Then, I open my eyes, and I'm in this Orleans Hotel room, alone, without you. I'm sad, but I'm happy because I now can see you whenever I want. I've read that the mind cannot distinguish what it imagines and thinks from what is real. So, I can visualize you and be with you anytime I want. That is the way I will get through the rest of my life.

When we left, I remember that my flight usually left first. As I boarded the plane I would stop at the end of the walkway, turn around and make sure we could still see each other, and our hands would go up in the final wave. On our last trip, I remember that final wave oh so well. I can see it now. It was March 19th at about 11:00 am. Oh, now it hurts so bad, for now I realize that no one ever knows when that final wave with someone is coming. Oh crap, I'm going to cry.

Once we went to Fry's in Las Vegas. You walked on one side of the store and I walked on the other and then we met in the back in the middle and then took each other to show what we found. When I go there now in Vegas, I just pretend you're on the other side and I guess, in a way, you are.

On this last trip I bought a pair of sunglasses that we had talked about on the previous trip. But in the past when I bought sunglasses with you, I would have you put them on so I could see what I would look like in them. That's a twin thing. This time I couldn't do that so it took me literally over thirty minutes to figure out which pair to get.

Of course, this trip to Las Vegas was different as you were not there. Or were you? Two surprising things related to this trip changed my perspective.

First, when I got home I had the feeling that I had just returned from Las Vegas and we had seen each other. I felt like you were there. I had the same energy and excitement and the same thoughts that I could hardly wait to go back to be together with you. Of course I was sad, and I was alone, and I missed you. But it was different. As I went about doing the things that we always did, and going to the places we go, I felt you were right with me. Sometimes I talked to you while I was driving. I did not spend time wallowing in pity. I worked on and edited the three different book projects we had been doing together. They were heavy, hard edits that took concentration. I could have never done this if I was depressed.

Second, when I was talking with Pamela on my cell phone after I returned, I commented it was always tough driving home after work because that's when I would talk to you about our day. When I said this, I suddenly realized that while I was on my trip in Las Vegas I never once had the thought I wish I could call you on the phone. Not once.

Now this is truly amazing to me because not being able to talk to you on the phone has been one of the hardest adjustments I've had to make. But during the entire time I was in Las Vegas I never had that thought. I had no reason to call you. It can only be for one reason. You were right there with me. I have no doubt that you were.

I can hardly wait to go back next year.

About the Photographs
Featured In This Book

YOU NEVER PLAN TO NEED PHOTOS for a book like this one. So, when you need them you have to hunt for them. Photos can tell their own story and sometimes capture feelings where words fail.

Don's amazing photographs were one of the things I discovered as I was packing up all of his possessions. When I got back, Pamela and I went through them to see what we could put in an electronic digital picture frame she had bought for me. One of Don's gifts was an astonishing "eye for a photo." We found countless photos that were evidence of this gift.

I remember growing up we used to watch "Man With A Camera" staring Charles Bronson. That's where Don first fell in love with photography. From those days in the seventh and eight grades, Don went on to photograph Robert Kennedy, Princess Diana and others. He also made several award winning films with his friend David Philips at Humboldt State University.

Photographs also capture what twins are all about. Now as I write this I realize that twins each have their own identity besides their "twin" identity. That's the identity that gets kids dressed in the same looking clothes, and the one most people pay attention to when twins are growing up. Don and I never paid much attention to this, but it was always there.

McKenzie Photo Album
Don and Ron as Babies

Don and Ron at Age 6 months. Can you guess which is which?
That's Don on the right and me on the left, or is it?

Everyone could not always tell us apart, but only my mother and father knew
which one was which. My mother always made certain (in most photographs)
that Don was on the right at all times. If you look hard enough at the photos,
it's really easy to tell who is who, until we got older, then every photo was
easily discernable between the two of us.

Every set of twins goes through the phase
of their parents dressing them alike. It sure
was fun until we got older and wanted to
establish our independence away from
anything identical. On trips to Las Vegas
we always made sure what shirt we were
wearing so we didn't meet at the airport at our arrival
looking the same. But it didn't matter, people always came up to us and said,
"Are you twins?" After my brother passed away, I wanted to wear his clothes,
as it gave me comfort. I wondered if other Twinless Twins (TT's) did the same
thing as me?

Don and Ron
the Happy Twin Brothers

Don and Ron at age 1

Don and Ron at age 2

Stork Brings Twins To McKenzie Family

Twin sons arrived at Klamath Valley hospital Thursday, June 27, for Mr. and Mrs. Max McKenzie, 1941 Painter. Both mother and sons are doing nicely. McKenzie is with the J. C. Penney company.

Mrs. McKenzie is the daughter of Mr. and Mrs. Chester Berman of Craig's. The twins are the McKenzies' first children.

Having Twins was big news in our town in the 40's, they did not have fertility drugs back then.

Don and Ron at age 3, did you notice our hands in this out-take shot?

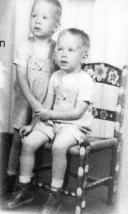

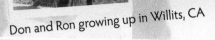

Don and Ron growing up in Willits, CA

Don and Ron as
Little Twin Cowboys

Age 5, weren't we the cutest? Our dad took this picture to give to our mom on Mother's Day.

Meet our wonderful parents: Alonzo Max and Janis Grace

First official family portrait at age 6 months.

Christmas with mom and dad at 18 months.

Growing up with my twin brother Don—the best brother in the whole world!

Our twin Christening photo.

Double the fun in our playpen!

Our first lesson in the vegetable garden.

We were even "identical twin thumb suckers" when we were little babies!

Enjoying our first ice cream cone, it was one of the few things our mom could not split in half as she did with most things we were given to eat.

Our 3rd Christmas together with new toy "telephones".... somebody forgot to tell mom we already had our own twin form of communications built-in! You can see our dog Mischa posing in the middle if you look close enough.

We always had fun adventures, and got great Christmas presents like toy machine guns!

Shared our horse rides too!

First twin sled ride together.

On our fifth Christmas we each got our own toy machine guns, guess it helped that dad managed the JCPenney store in town too! A few Christmases later we also got the genuine Red Ryder 200-shot Carbine Action Air Rifle!

First fishing trip!

Early "Twin Hugs"!

We always knew it was our grandfather playing Santa Claus!

Don and Ron as
Hopalong Cassidy, and
the Lone Ranger and Tonto!

Little did I know this picture
foreshadowed that I
was also to become
the Lone Twin someday.

Don and Ron as "Hip" Californians

Can you guess which is which? Did you notice our arms?
Photo by: Patti Stammer

Don and Ron
Always Best Friends

Don and Ron
back-to-back
in Colorado.

Don and Ron in the Pacific State Beach on our
many trips to visit mom.

We got to
share and
spend our
40th Birthday
together in
Chicago,
when Don
came to visit
Pam & me
for a while.
Her sister
Nancy made
us a summer
BBQ party to
celebrate.
We always
had fun.

LORDY
LORDY
LOOK
WHO'S
40

Don and Ron in Las Vegas
Hacienda and MGM Grand

Don and Ron at The Hacienda in Las Vegas, did you notice our hands?
We are so easy to tell apart now, Don has the beard of course!
We were there to see Lance Burton before he got the Monte Carlo gig.

Don and Ron in Las Vegas in front of the "better" lion front which they were
tearing down. MGM was the site of our first Fargo Blue Mystery Novel,
Poolside Sting. It is rare to find books penned by identical twins.
I don't think there are many mystery novel twin authors.

Don and Ron in Las Vegas
Luxor and Monte Carlo

Don and Ron in front of The Luxor in Las Vegas, on one of our many location scouting trips for background material in the Fargo Blue Mystery Novel Series. We actually mapped out 13 novels together in the Fargo Blue series. I plan on continuing to see our mutual dream of authorship stay alive. Don wrote many screenplays, he was good at it too. Did you notice our hands?

Don and Ron
MCKENZIE
POOLSIDE STING
Texas Hold 'Em!
A Fargo Blue Mystery

Don and Ron
MCKENZIE
COYOTE TRAP
A Straight Up Bet!
LAS VEGAS
A Fargo Blue Mystery

Don and Ron in Las Vegas working on the Las Vegas Life publicity article for Fargo Blue Mystery novel, Poolside Sting. I was lucky enough to have received his autograph on our first published novel.

Don and Ron in the Las Vegas Life publicity piece and at Area 51

Don and Ron originally published the Fargo Blue story under another title: Las Vegas Comp, Murder at the Emerald Towers. The premise of the book series Fargo Blue, was that the detective gets comped by the big casinos, to solve the mystery. Fargo has many places he frequents and a girlfriend who's a dancer at the Tropicana.

And yes, you guessed it, Fargo's future adventures just had to take him into AREA 51, at Nellis AFB, a highly restricted government area where Don is pictured. We had lunch together at the little A'le'Inn!

Don as Senior Editor for Paramount Studios Entertainment Tonight

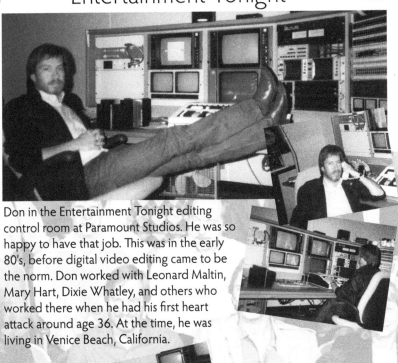

Don in the Entertainment Tonight editing control room at Paramount Studios. He was so happy to have that job. This was in the early 80's, before digital video editing came to be the norm. Don worked with Leonard Maltin, Mary Hart, Dixie Whatley, and others who worked there when he had his first heart attack around age 36. At the time, he was living in Venice Beach, California.

Don in one of the news editing rooms he worked both in San Francisco, KGO and Los Angeles, KTLA. The biggest story at the time was the Patty Hearst kidnapping which he cut for the national news feed. He had more press and photography badges than anyone I ever knew!

Don on the back lot at Paramount. Somehow I think he is still there with the rest of the late stars who are screenwriting, directing & producing in Hollywood heaven!

Don in Japan

This black and white photo in Japan was Don's favorite of himself, doing one of the things he loved best — working with his camera!

Don in Japan with his good friend Saho, and the cultures of the city and busy making films of course!

Don, Saho, Ron and friend in Japan in 1984.

Don with his good friend and Japanese interpreter, Saho in 1983.

Don wearing his Paramount Studios sweatshirt pictured with the Japanese Emperor in 1988. It was the Emperor's last public visit.

Don as writer, photographer, video man, news editor, he had some real special talent and a passion for photography. He loved his three year stay in Japan.

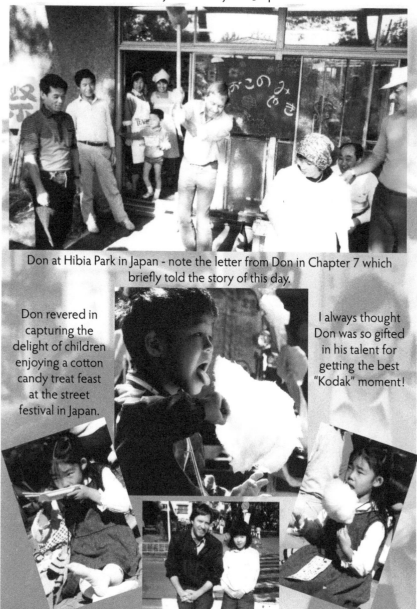

Don at Hibia Park in Japan - note the letter from Don in Chapter 7 which briefly told the story of this day.

Don revered in capturing the delight of children enjoying a cotton candy treat feast at the street festival in Japan.

I always thought Don was so gifted in his talent for getting the best "Kodak" moment!

Don's love for adventure also took him to other faraway places like Boracay and of course, Hong Kong!

Don in Boracay - wearing a polo shirt with the logo of the Chicago Bears, and pictured with a friend of course!

Don in Hong Kong, looking like a tai-pan! We had a great time there together!

One of Don's proudest moments was when his job at Paramount afforded him the chance to buy a nice, shiny new BMW!

More pictures of my brother Don in
Las Vegas, the Hoover Dam, and yes, even Starbucks.
We lived for those adventurous annual trips!

More pictures of my brother Don in
Las Vegas, Red Rock Canyon, In-N-Out Burger.
Little did I know that all these treasured
photographs were going to end up in this book.

Absolutely nothing can ever beat the wonderful memories I have of Don and me on vacation in Las Vegas doing our twin brotherly thing and our fave: Fargo Blue detective book-scouting, trying new local restaurants and playing catch.

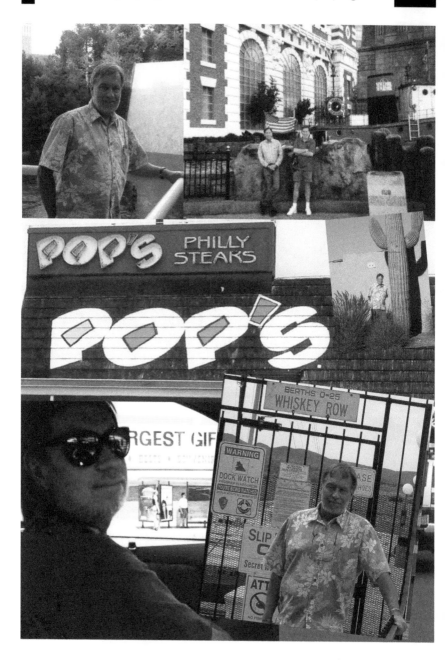

Don inside his used Book Store in Oregon with his other best friend, ever constant book scout and faithful companion, Amigo.

Photographs of my brother Don in recent years when setting up the Book Stores he owned and doing Antique Co-ops in Lincoln City, Oregon. He was always doing what he loved best, and being surrounded by books was sheer joy to him.

This headshot of Don was one of the last photographs for his E-Zine article column in mid 2008.

September 7, 2008, the fateful day that left me half a man, and half a twin, because half of me died along with him.

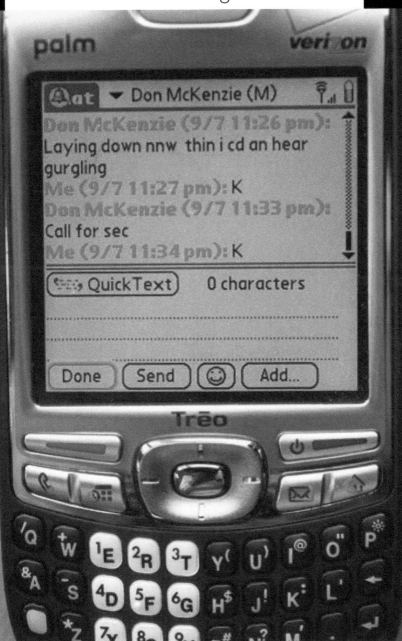

One thing about Las Vegas aside from it being a 24/7 town. Everything, I mean everything changes constantly. Even the infamous neon sign is now surrounded by a park-like setting designed for tourist picture-taking off South Las Vegas Boulevard. There is a small parking lot and room for two Las Vegas tour buses. Somehow I know my brother's spirit lives there, and that is why I will continue to honor his wishes for me to go there, and retire there, for as long as my health and legs and Fargo Blue's Mystery adventures will take me; until I am laid to rest alongside Don and our parents not very far from the Ridgewood Ranch in Ukiah, California.

Seven
The Heartbreak Of It All

I DON'T KNOW WHAT it's like not to be a twin. I mean, I still see you with me in my mind. I see you happy and not afraid. How does a non-twin exist? Who do they talk to?

I just realized you don't have to go to the dentist anymore. That's really not fair. I say this as I sit here in great pain. I just had one emergency root canal and I have another one next week.

Don't worry Don, I'm okay, although I'm still devastated by your passing. I will find my way; I will find my place to be that allows a little ray of sunshine. But Don, we must promise each other, you don't worry about me and I won't worry about you. With that said, let me state that I know I'll still worry about you and you will still worry about me. That's just a twin thing.

Don, what makes me so sad is it was a regular day for you – nothing special to do. Get up, play with and feed Amigo. Do final prep for show and head to Starbucks on the way to your work at the antique show. We talked several times that day. You mentioned the acid reflux and I said get a Coke and you thought that was a good idea. You were complaining of some discomfort but thought it was just acid reflux. You stopped and got some calcium tablets. You also put a nitro patch on and chewed aspirin. When you got home, you went inside and never unpacked your van. You tried to calm yourself down. You poured some wine and sipped on it. We talked several times and then I went to bed and left my phone on. You

47

texted me a couple of times and then another one—your last—that said "call for a sec" and I did.

When we talked you said you were really stressed out and I said you had to get to the hospital. You agreed and got the car, put Amigo in the back and we talked as you drove. Neither one of us thought this was severe. When you got to the hospital you called as you were filling out the paperwork, and said "I just want to get past this and get to Vegas." Those were your last words to me. About forty-five minutes later I got the call. I was downstairs on the couch frantic with worry when the phone buzzed and my world changed. A regular day with no threats of death. Is this how everyone's last day is? I don't know.

Hey, do you remember when we investigated law school? I think about that and our trips to UNLV all the time. In the end we each made the right decision. If we would have had different guidance and more money I think we would have made good attorneys. Remember the Summary Judgment I wrote? I got you on that one! But you know, at least we tried. I loved the conversations we had about this and many other topics sitting outside the Starbucks on Sahara Avenue. You know the one.

I decided to start exercising at the gym. Last week as I was working out I listened to music from our favorite piano player in Las Vegas. When one song came on and I realized it was the music that was playing when I was alone with you at the mortuary. The song was Memories. I told you then that I have a lot of memories of our life together, especially our trips to Las Vegas and our writing sessions.

A hundred times a day something reminds me of you. Is it you trying to tell me you're all right? I believe so.

I am both sad and grateful that our last day together was a regular day, and that we had those last conversations like many other times, not knowing they would be our last. Oh Don, I miss you so much.

Tonight Pam and I watched a film named Melinda and Melinda, written and directed by Woody Allen, that I shipped home from your large DVD film library. It was the first time we sat down to watch a movie together since you died. Pam picked it out and said: "This one was the first one I saw in the stack when I first opened the big box, and we haven't seen it." To my surprise, in the film was a clear and distinguishable sign from you to me. That happens to me all the time now. It was at the end of the movie and the character named "Sy" played by Wallace Shawn, said: "You never know; it can end just like that." Simultaneously, he snapped his fingers and the screen went completely black. In addition, ironically, when the movie first debuted in 2004, one of the trailer taglines was: "Life can be a comedy or a tragedy; it all depends on how you look at it."

Remember when we used to sit on the fence posts waiting for dad to drive up the hill in Willits so we could open the gate. I say this knowing that you remembered things about growing up that I had forgotten. Together we made our memories complete. Now half of my memory is gone.

The other night I had a dinner with a friend. It was difficult because I kept thinking that after dinner I could not call you on the way home. I cried almost all the way home in the car. I couldn't stop the tears, and I didn't want to, as it was all I could do at that time.

Don, I am so sorry that I left you alone. Please know that everything is okay at that I am well now. We must both be happy.

I wonder if there will ever be a day when I will say at the end of the day, "I really enjoyed this day. It was a good day and I am happy."

I was watching TV and they showed a whale shooting out of the water, rolling over and slipping back into the ocean. I immediately thought of when we went whale watching with Saho and it got so cold when we were coming back. We saw the whales dive and splash. It was a good day. Things like that happen all the time to me now. I see something and think of you. I like it. It's good for me.

Don, do you remember the time when we went to the movies with Drew Barrymore in Hollywood? Well, I admit that she did sit in a different row and had a friend with her, but we were at the show with her. When we got outside we saw Susan Anton. That was a good night in Westwood, wasn't it?

Remember our talks about how we wished someone would have given us a "life plan" when we were ready to graduate from high school. Someone should have sat us down and said here is your "Financial Medical Life Plan." It includes:

a) a continuous non-touchable savings;
b) a medical plan that is on-going;
c) a staged retirement plan;
d) taking one retirement planning seminar a year starting at age 35, and
e) you both shall remain close and be the executor of the will and estate of the other, making sure that families were taken care of;
f) that these rules shall never be broken.

With that said, we would have been told to go do anything you want. Would that have made a difference in our life? This kind of planning is what every person should do, but maybe it is even more important for twins because of the trauma of the separation of a union that began in the womb.

Don, now I worry when and where I will die. I am not scared, but am I going to end up in a rest home not knowing anyone? The week before you died you said that you were worried that we would not be in the same retirement home.

An event Pam and I went to the other evening reminded me of how much you loved the theater. We were invited by a gentleman associated with the Wheaton Grand Theatre. After a cocktail reception, a set of doors opened and we went into a room that sat a hundred people. The lights dimmed, the curtain opened and organ music started to build. The organ that slid out from the wall was one of the five original Robert Morton "Wonder" Organs. It had been relocated from Loew's King's Theatre in Brooklyn to Wheaton. It was huge and in perfect condition. After playing some music and explaining the history of the organ a Laurel and Hardy silent film was shown and accompanied by the organ. It also reminded me of when we saw the production of Mr. Roberts in Las Vegas. Don, you would have loved to see this organ and the film, but I believe you were there with us.

Don, I worried about you a lot. I wanted you to be happy, to have everything 'perfect'. You had to struggle so much, but you never gave up. I could sense your happiness when I had to pack your belongings and clear your place. But I also knew of your sadness. I know what you wanted, what you deserved, and what you were fighting for all these years. But, you're in heaven now, and I think you will be rewarded because you were a fine, honest man who always thought the best of people. Even if someone hurt you, you still cared about them. I worry a lot, but I shouldn't as you are with God and He will take care of you.

I know that I was an anchor in your world as much as you were an anchor in mine. I loved helping you; I looked forward to it as it meant it was one step closer to happiness.

Don, as I have said before, I have without question been deeply hurt by your passing and the seemingly unfairness of it all. But I now realize the hurt is only an expression of the love I have for you. But you will never leave my mind, so we will spend them together after all. You are with me always.

All I know is when I look in the mirror I see you and I hurt.

Don, I am in another meeting. I was thinking of you and and speed dialed you on my phone just so I could see your name come up. Oh, it hurts me so much that now you can't answer. It hurts deep down inside. Why, I keep asking? Why couldn't we spend our retirement years together? I can still see you walking towards me and you are happy and we are together. Oh my, this seems so unfair.

Each time I think of you, the memories resurface. Do you remember when you left about five in the morning to drive that RV to the movie set and as soon as you went around a corner on the highway the huge container with gallons of hot coffee dumped right on to the floor? You had to stop, clean up the RV and get more coffee.

Tonight I thought about how we walked the streets of New York at different times for different reasons. You hustled diamonds on 47th street and I was at two different meetings. Afterwards I stayed to explore. I walked Central Park, and saw two stage plays on Broadway.

* * *

I just returned from unpacking your storage locker. It took three 10-hour days to go through about 450 boxes.

I was quite comfortable sitting there on a box surrounded by all your things. It constantly brought back memories of when we were growing up and all of the things you did in your life. I sent home about fifteen boxes of things that I will go through and enjoy.

I planned the trip to occur with the Theater Arts reunion and a memorial for Richard Rothrock. I contacted William Word prior to going out and he asked me to stop by. I found his house, met William and Carol and we all sat in the kitchen and talked. It was a strange meeting, but it felt more like a reunion, as though I had known William and Carol forever. William said it felt like he was talking to Don. I met up with them again at a cocktail reception and we had dinner together at Luzmila's Mexican Restaurant. That's where you took me several years earlier. When we walked in I remembered exactly where we sat.

William, Carol and I talked about the time you and William had dinner with actress Shirley MacLaine to discuss one of William's films that she was interested in. That must have been a lot of fun.

The night I arrived I had dinner with David and LouAnna Phillips, Jan Rothrock, at Patrick Conlin and Carol Davis' home.

Another night I reminisced at dinner with David and LouAnna Phillips. I even had a photo shoot with your dog Amigo, who is now called "The Dude". It is one of my favorite photos and it's on the back cover of this book.

After I finished on Friday I had time before the reception to drive out to Moonstone Beach where I had met Dave and LouAnna for dinner. That's the beach you took me to probably thirty-five years ago. I walked the beach alone just like you had done so many times. I felt comfortable and happy there because I found the beach—something I never thought I could do.

The whole trip went perfectly. The Arcata part ended when I arrived at the Van Duzer Theater and saw the memorial on the wall of past Alumni of your Theater Arts Department. The photos I had sent were there of you in Japan and your editing studio. You looked good; but you should not have been on that memorial wall.

After seeing that, and walking around your beloved campus, I hit the road, drove to Ukiah and saw OUR headstone with both of our names on it. I stopped at Greg's vineyard and then headed toward San Francisco. The first stop was Union Square where I parked and went to Lefty O'Doul's for dinner. Then I walked past the ACT Theater and the Curran Theater and where the old Geary Street bookstore was that we used to go with mom and dad.

The next morning I drove past where mom used to live, and then went to Draeger's in San Mateo for coffee. That's where mom loved to go, and where we took her to so many times. Then I drove to Kepler's by Stanford University, and to Foothill in Los Altos Hills. I drove back to the airport, and caught a flight home.

It's all done. Everything is taken care of and you no longer have a locker in Arcata. It's all in my basement.

Letters from Don
On A Garage Sale in Japan

"Today was interesting. I woke up to marching bands and drums. So after my coffee I grabbed my camera and headed out. It turned out to be a huge garage sale and festival. There were people everywhere, and I took photos of kids eating cotton candy. I ended up at a place where they had sort of a stage where they make a special soup with dough. A guy takes a whack at the dough with a huge wooden sledgehammer and then a girl moves the dough. As the guy swings everyone yells and screams. I started talking to someone, which means I nod my head when they speak so they think I understand them. It turns out I had agreed to be the next one on the stage. I started to say Iiya, iiya, which is no in Japanese. So now there are over one hundred people yelling and screaming for me to do it and I know I am in deep shit.

So I take my ET jacket off, give my camera to someone to take a photo of me, and got up on stage and could not believe I had gotten myself into this situation. They handed me the wooden sledgehammer and I bowed to him and the crowd went crazy. I started to beat the dough, and each time I hit it the crowd cheered. Everyone either really appreciated my effort or I was the joke of the day. I don't know which, but my new rule is not to nod my head like I understand what is being said."

Letters from Don
On Working in Japan

"I'm in a suit and tie today as I went and auditioned
for a fashion model job. I changed into the clothes I was
to model in a large room where everyone was hanging out.
Then I had to do a runway walk, which I thought was fun."

Letters from Don
On Working in Hollywood

"I'm swamped with work. I find out this weekend
about Streets of San Francisco. It's down to a producer
meeting. If it's a go I move on to a second draft of the script.
Besides that I have a story conference meeting at
Universal on the movie idea I have named **Switch.**
I have never made any pitch at this level before.
I have to go in and convince them that I have the
greatest story idea in the world."

Eight
Birthday For Two

TODAY IS YOUR BIRTHDAY - JUNE 27. Happy Birthday Don.

It is also my birthday, and that is where I have the problem. This is the first birthday without you. We have been separated many times on our birthdays, but even when you were living in Japan, we always managed to talk.

I'm trying to understand this. You are the older twin, but now I have lived longer, so does that now make me the older twin? I think the answer is no. You are still older as you are still with me everyday.

Ironically, how can you have a cake that says Happy Birthday, if it isn't? I chose not to have a cake and I celebrate our day by doing the things I like to do. I cried the night before, but I didn't cry on our birthday.

Don, remember when we were in Las Vegas and it was our sixtieth birthday. We timed it so we were in our hotel room with our favorite view and a bottle of wine and we were toasting. I then said that right now you are sixty years old, and I'm in my late fifties. Of course this lasted for only nine minutes or so, but I never let up. Here, can I get you a cane? You better watch the amount of wine you drink. Here, let me help you with that. You loved it.

That was a special trip, because we wanted to be together on our sixtieth birthday. We usually went earlier to avoid the desert heat, but this trip was different, at the end of June and the first part of July. It was really hot. We bought an ice cooler for the car and two six packs of water. We also bought one of those sun-shades for the front window of the rental car to keep the steering wheel from getting so hot you couldn't touch it when we got in.

One of the things we had talked about was each of us buying a new gaming system. We discussed it by phone, looked at the games and decided we would get the PS3 system. On our trip in September 2008 we were each supposed to buy two games. Then when we got home we would buy the actual gaming unit, hook it up and play. Of course that trip never happened as you passed away ten days before we were supposed to leave.

On my trip this year I went ahead with our plan. I purchased several games, and when I got home I purchased the PS3 gaming unit. But I waited until our birthday to play. I had it all set up and ready to go, but I didn't put a game unit in until Saturday morning, on our birthday.

By carrying through with this plan it makes it as though you were with me. I know exactly what would have happened. We would have been on the phone all morning as we hooked it up and began to play. Twins can do things together even though they are miles or continents apart. Twins can also do things together even when one has passed on. The other twin is still there. Don, you are with me right now on our birthday.

I went out earlier this week and bought two small special presents. When I got home I wrapped them, and marked them: "To Ron, from Don. Happy Birthday." I opened them this evening. That's just the way it is. I will always have a Christmas present from Don, and I will always have a birthday present from you. I will also continue to buy Don presents.

I got a call today on my birthday from Yuliya Olvy, a friend of Pam and I who used to work at ARCON. I knew she was taking her LEED AP exam today, and she was so excited that she passed her test. Of course she didn't know it was my birthday, and I told her that was the best birthday gift anyone could give me to hear the good news. I was so happy for her on this achievement, and it meant something to me that she called me. She, or course, was saddened to hear it was my first birthday without my twin brother. But I told her I was fine, and I was ever so happy for her.

Yuliya is a good friend. Friends do make a difference, and helping someone achieve their goals makes you feel good, particularly when it is so easy to feel bad.

Happy Birthday, Don.

Letters from Don
On Directing

"I got named as the director for a British Chamber of Commerce Television show. The project is going well and I found out that the studio was really impressed with my direction of the taping as they had never worked with an American Director before. They were quite impressed with how I was able to direct and cut the story and said it was extraordinary. I was the floor director, meaning I directed when people spoke and the placement of people; basically how people said things. I created the scene. Then I went to the control booth where I called the show. . .roll tape. . . camera one . . .camera three, and so on. I had no trouble leading the people through the taping. Of course this comes from cutting hundreds of news stories and stories for ET. I have a sense of story telling and timing that makes it work."

Nine
One Year Alone

TODAY IS ONE YEAR TO THE DATE that you passed away. I'm not working today. I'm spending the day with you in every way that I can. I loved you so much; I miss you so much. I am half a man, half a brother, and half a twin. Half of my soul is gone.

I often think of the fact that we could communicate huge amounts of information by just the nod of a head. If we were in a group we could still communicate without talking. I miss that.

I have said this, but I'm going to say it again, I still wish for an email, to hear your voice on the phone, to hear my phone tell me there is a text message waiting, to see you at the airport; to start our trip on that magical drive into Las Vegas, getting our room, and the first glass of wine. I miss just sitting with you and being together. I miss falling asleep with knowing you are in the same room and that we are both safe, happy and okay for now. I miss that first breakfast and all the firsts of the trips. But the main thing I miss is just being with you knowing that we are once again ONE.

I wish for us to be together again; it will happen when I get to heaven.

This past year has been a terribly long year and I think of you all the time. Nothing has changed. My heart aches and I cry and I try to be brave, but it is tough to be brave alone when you were once part of someone else.

Don, my goal is to succeed in everything I try and to make a difference. I am the last of this McKenzie clan and now I represent you, dad and mom. It helps my pain.

We often talked about having minimal guidance when we were growing up. Perhaps it was because dad passed away when we were so young. Mom did the best she could do, but it was more of a protective response. We talked all the time about how great it would have been to share our business experiences with dad and to get his advice. But more than that, there was no guidance about being a twin. Parents really don't understand the closeness of twins, so they don't know what to do. We did a great job, but no one said that one of you is in for a heartbreak that will impact the rest of your life. Or, told us to stay close together because the times with each other are when the two of you are one.

I've been thinking about this idea of guidance and wonder if it would have made a difference in our lives.

Don, I still cry, but it's no longer because of sadness; it's because I understand. I wish I didn't understand; I wish I could just cry.

Letters from Don
On Golf in College

"Maybe we could play a game of golf Monday afternoon
down at Fremont. Get there about 4:30, bounce
a check and play nine holes."

Letters from Don
On Golf

"I am very anxious to get to Chicago and spend some time having lunches and playing some golf. I'm ready to go out and tackle the course and see what we can do. I want to be out on the golf course hitting those sand traps. I will hit it straight down the middle and then go into the water on my second shot. I will walk away with my usually lucky seven or the dreaded snowman."

Ten
Don Talks To Ron

FOR SOME THIS NEXT SECTION MAY SEEM STRANGE.
But most twins will recognize the ability of one twin to know exactly
what the other would say or do in a given situation. This was also
created with the help of Megan Beach, who talked extensively with
me after Don's death.

*"Ron, I'm so sorry I left you. I don't know why God took me away
from you. I'm so hurt on the inside as I think about how you helped
me with my life and how our last moments unfolded.*

*You were there for me right up until the end. I was really
concerned when I texted you so late at night. You got me to go to
the hospital and talked to me on the phone as I drove there. Then we
talked again for the last time when I got inside.*

*I was scared, Ron. I know you could hear it in my voice and you got
me to do what I needed to do. But both of us never had any idea it
was going to lead to my passing. I started to have more trouble once
I got in the emergency room, then started to have difficulty breathing
and then I passed out.*

*I never told you that when I had my first heart attack I floated just
above me and watched them work on me. Ron, I can't tell you if that
happened this time. I told Megan Beach about the first time, and I now
know that she has become your friend.*

McKenzie

I don't remember anything after I passed out, but up to that point I was so scared and worried about you. I was thinking of what was going to happen to me, and at the same time, I was thinking of you and how much I love you and our times together. I am thankful for no pain, but I was willing to accept the pain if it meant a fighting chance for us to stay together. Ron, I fought as hard as I could for us. I am sorry I did not make it. My anguish of our separation is incomprehensible.

My last thoughts were of you and how much I loved you. I also thought about how your life was going to be without me. I also thought about the huge disappointment of not taking our trip that was just days away. I thought of all of our happy times and of our entire life together as far back as we can remember. I thought of all of that, but my main thought was my overwhelming concern for leaving you alone. I am so sorry. I am so, so sorry, Ron.

There were so many things I wanted to tell you in those last few seconds, so I am doing it now, through you. First, I loved you with all my heart and soul as much as anyone could love someone. You were what completed my world – it is what I lived for, the you and I – the twins.

You worked so hard with me in the last two years to help me get out of the situation I was in, and to leave behind all the people that took advantage of me. Your unrelenting, unquestioning support and help was what I needed so much. You were there with no questions asked. It hurt me, but it was the help I needed. I would have done the same for you, and I know you knew that.

I remember in Humboldt, when we worked on our projects and you worked weekends for over a year to come up with our eBooks and marketing concept. You learned all that software and figured out all those things about marketing on the Internet. It meant so much to me that you helped me.

Who Moved The Sun?

In the end I was happy. Yes, I wanted more than what I had achieved in my life. But as you pointed out, and as we proved, it is not the material things and money that make you happy; it is the relationships between people, their love for each other that gives them the means to enjoy the simple things in life and tackle problems together. As you said, we are the true millionaires.

As you pointed out to me, people as well as large companies took advantage of my good nature and they stole from me and damaged me in many ways. But when I said I wanted to move back to my college town in Northern California you were right there saying "Good decision – let's work out a plan."

I had a lot of sadness in my life after I moved but you pointed out that was the past – we have our whole future ahead of us. That's when we went to work. That's when we had such a great time and had our first business planning meeting in Las Vegas. It was all coming together. It was also to be our last business meeting.

But I was happy as I had a future even though all my retirement plans had been taken from me – in effect, I had nothing. But you were right at my side making sure I was doing the right things to keep it all coming together.

Our next Las Vegas trip was only days away and I wanted so badly to see you and hug you so we could be together, but it was taken away from us. I just wanted to be together away from everything. Just you and I. As we talked, the next trip was always to be the best.

Ron, as we discussed on the last several trips, it is now up to you to take that trip. You will not be alone; for we agreed that whoever dies first, the other one would be right at the other's side. Ron, you must go; and now we know that it is I who will be there with you all the time, just as I am right now. In a matter of an hour, I left you by yourself. You had to make all my burial arrangements and you did a great job. Talking with Pamela on the phone and evaluating the situation you came up with the perfect plan. Being cremated and buried between mom and dad was perfect. We know you will be buried next to me. And best of all, we are going to share one headstone. Perfect. In the end we will be together with mom and dad.

I am so sorry I left you; I worry so much about you. I want you to have a good life. I know you will think of me constantly. But I am here, and I am happy, and I will protect you. I want you to be happy; enjoy your life Ron. For in the end, the real end, we will be together again. I cannot tell you about this place but since we are twins, you already know what to expect.

Ron, please find an island for yourself, an island in the sun, your new sun, for the old one has been moved. Make it a place, where you can go and be happy with memories of our wonderful life together. I want you to live and enjoy life, and laugh. But, remember, we will still cry together.

I am forever grateful for our friendship and brotherly love that led to all the special moments we had together. From playing together when we were kids, to all of our meetings in San Francisco, our time in Los Angeles, the great fun we had in Hong Kong and Japan, our trips to Las Vegas and all of the places we explored, and all of the other millions of things we did together. Of course, the really important part was just being together; it didn't quite matter where. It's where you took care of me, and I took care of you. Our great secret was when we were together, we were ONE, and it will be that way, again, someday.

Have a wonderful life; I am with you all the time. If you need something just ask me, and I will give you all the answers.

Who Moved The Sun?

I love you and I miss you and I'm okay. Be happy, and cry for me when you must, and I will cry with you."

See you again someday, Love, Don, Your Twin

P.S. I was the one that made you buy the matching Urn so we could have the same one. That's just how it works with us.

Letters from Don
On Diamonds

"If I owned a jewelry store I would show loose diamonds in the window and under the display glass in their paper folders spilling out. For some reason this to most people is a secret world and when a diamond is unwrapped it's like being involved in the mystery and intrigue that have followed diamonds through the course of history. When I was hustling diamonds I always made a big deal of unwrapping and the presentation. Jewelry stores could easily increase their sales with a little drama instead of showing two-hundred wedding rings in a showcase. They all look the same to most people."

Letters from Don
Chicago Haymarket

"No word yet on the Mary Tyler Moore show. I expect that I will hear in about a week. This is the best script I have written. The Haymarket story that is centered in Chicago went back to Warner Brothers through my agent who said an estimate was made by Sun Productions that it would cost six to eight million to bring to the screen. No words on the Killer book yet."

Eleven
Twin Hugs

THERE ARE MANY LIFE LESSONS in this book, which is about separation. To twins, even though they may live miles apart, they are closer together than most persons. Twins always find a way to be together as my brother and I did. We were really ONE even though we were many miles apart. However, final separation is a very difficult thing. It is something that no surviving twin would ever wish on their twin or anyone else. It is a painful never-ending life adjustment that few understand, particularly the outside people around the twin.

Even though Don passed away, we are still ONE. That is essentially the situation that is addressed in this book. Now, though, there is extreme and agonizing loneliness combined with a sense that part of you is gone. I am not kidding when I say this. How do you live with half a soul? Now I view myself as alone in the world even though I have a wonderful wife and many friends. Many twins are lucky enough to have a spouse that understands and supports the twinship completely. This is not really the same as non-twins who have a very close relationship with someone. They don't have a part of what was with them in the womb missing, and that makes all the difference in the world.

Besides helping twins, this book is designed to also help parents of twins, counselors, friends, or other people who grieve for a passed loved one. Several points in this journal may help make a difference for that twin, that parent, that counselor, that priest, or that friend.

71

First, twins when they reach a certain age must start to address the "what if" questions. When it is best to talk about this is totally up to the twins. A parent cannot force this on them, but they can look for signs that the time is right. It is a tough subject to bring up, and there probably is never an easy time for it. But it's never too early to start thinking about it.

This conversation between twins should lead directly to the topic of what happens when one of them dies. How is the other going to survive? The truth is, this is easily brushed off, but the reality of the situation is that when a twin does die it's an incredible shock to the remaining twin. The real shock of it and the loss and sadness may also occur many years later when the survivor least expects it.

The twins, at the right age, should plan something to tie them together when one is not there. Of course, they have millions of twin experiences to give them memories, but if they can plan something together that the survivor carries out, it will give both of them a sense of comfort. In our case, we agreed that the surviving twin will go to Las Vegas to make the very same trip that they would have together, knowing that the other twin is still there. That has given me a sense of comfort far beyond my imagination. Other examples might be:

A walk in a park on a fall day every year where they had both walked together.

A walk by the ocean at their secret beach.

A trip someplace or maybe a local spot they had talked about exploring together but never were able to make.

A visit to where they grew up together.

Enjoying a twin's favorite meal.

A trip to a place or a city where they shared a good time.

In my case, I did all of these and will continue to do them. Whatever it is, the most important part is to talk about it ahead of time. If a twin has passed away, then the surviving twin can develop their own place to be to find comfort.

There are other situations, such as when a twin dies at birth, or before birth. Some parents react as if that twin did not exist. Also, there are cases when twins do not know they are a twin because they were separated at or shortly after birth. But it has been proven that the surviving twin, who is unaware of being a twin, will have the same kinds of feelings of loneliness and heartbreak when their twin dies but will not know why. In these situations, there is no opportunity to discuss the what if questions. So what do they do? They simply, do what twins do best – make up something.

If you are a twin, use your feelings to develop something that you and only you can do alone so you can be with your twin. If you absolutely love having lunch in the park, then have lunch in the park by yourself, because if you love it, then your twin would also love it, because they know it makes you happy.

As I have mentioned, occasionally when a twin dies the parents pretend the other twin never existed. I have read instances of parents removing all photos of the twin or even not allowing the surviving twin to go to the funeral. Of course, this is a terrible injustice and something the twin must come to terms with when they are older. It is the saddest of saddest situations.

Parents need to understand the depth of the twin's loss. In the case of identical twins, they came from the same seed. But all twins, fraternal and identical, share the same womb. It now has been shown that twins in the womb do a tremendous amount of touching and cuddling. This is where it all starts.

As an example, when Don and I were walking down the street, we only felt comfortable when he was on my left side. When he walked on my right side it just felt wrong. He felt the same way. This is probably because of how we were in mom's womb. It is those kinds of things that carry on later in life that a twin deals with that others never think about.

So a parent must learn to recognize and help the child understand that the twin will be with him or her forever – but physically only until one twin dies. If it is tough for an adult to adjust to the loss of someone close to them, imagine how terribly difficult it is for a child to cope with a twin loss.

Friends and family need to recognize the special sensitivity surrounding a twin's death. It is nearly impossible for a non-twin to understand the enormity of this kind of loss to a twin. The pain is at times unbearable, and nearly overwhelming.

Some professional counselors will understand the twin's loss, but it's my understanding that there are very few counselors that are fully trained in twin loss.

Married couples face a similar situation. They should also sit down to talk about what happens when one spouse is gone. Talk openly about it: Will you be all right without me? What could you do during those times when you feel alone and need help? If you have these kinds of understandings upfront, it will be very helpful, especially when one spouse dies suddenly. It does not lighten the enormity of the pain of death, but it will help the survivor.

Plan for death. Get your paperwork in order. Have all of those documents filled out as soon as possible. I am not an attorney but things such as a revocable trust, and other documents can be changed as you move through life. Dying without a will, or intestate, is not what you want, because it may put the survivors through years of potential court and legal battles if there is any protest or disagreement.

For a twin, you must learn to live with an empty space that cannot be replaced by anyone else. Your twin will always be there, but the space that was his or hers is now empty. My twin is my angel and I am peace with that.

Letters from Don
On Mom's Letters

"My letters are probably longer than mom's. If we get her a computer let's tell her she can't do word processing. Imagine the letters we would get if she had word processing to work with! We wouldn't be able to afford the paper."

Letters from Don
Movie of the Week

"Not much happening here. I've been working on story ideas. This Tuesday I have a meeting with Stanley Roberts, Vice President of NBC in charge of Movie of the Week, who wanted to meet me after reading Night Puppet. He didn't want to buy the script but wanted to see if he could help me because of my writing."

Twelve
The Conversations

THE CONVERSATION BETWEEN MY BROTHER AND I about one of us dying took place as we sat having a glass of wine in our room at the Orleans Hotel overlooking the strip in Las Vegas. It went like this:

Ron: *Some day one of us may die, and we must be ready for that.*

Don: *We're healthy for the most part. I figure we'll start having problems in our early seventies, and that's when there will be issues.*

Ron: *Still, you never know when your number comes up. Maybe some other driver runs a red light and you're history.*

Don: *True. I guess we must understand that the one left must keep on going.*

Ron: *I think if that ever happens the one left should come back to Las Vegas and do the trip exactly like we normally do the trip. They should do it as often as they like or need to.*

Don: *That's good. And the best part is the one that died will be right by the other's side. It will be the same trip.*

Ron: *So you think we should do that?*

Don: *Yes.*

77

What I have learned is that this kind of conversation needs to be expanded. It's a tough conversation that no one wants to have. But it's important for everyone to do it. Married couples, or people who live with significant others or friends, should have it. But for twins, this conversation is critical.

Following is how the rest of our conversation should have gone.

Ron: *But more than that, Don, we must really talk about how enormously difficult it will be for the twin left behind – the survivor if you will.*

Don: *You're right. I think that being twinless will be the toughest challenge ever. It will be so difficult for the one left behind. We just have to remember that we can't stop living at this point. We must move forward and work at having a good life.*

Ron: *Yes. But that will be hard. Perhaps what we need to do is to understand that we have all these projects we're working on. The one that is left behind can continue with these projects, and in a way, it will be as if we are working together.*

Don: *Well, I believe that because we are twins, we will always be at the other's side.*

Ron: *You know, another thing we can do is to visit other places we enjoyed. We have been a lot of places together, and if we go there it will be like we're together again, just like the plan for Las Vegas.*

Don: *I agree. Another thing to do is when you are feeling bad about being left alone, hold your hand over your eyes and imagine the other one someplace, like the bridge between the New York, New York and the MGM Grand Casinos. Or the footbridge we were at in Hong Kong* *the day of the Dragon Boat Races. Or, when we were standing at the Peak in Hong Kong. When you see the other one there, wave, and the other will wave back.*

Ron: *Right, and as we learned in quantum physics the mind doesn't know the difference, so it's real for the person with their eyes covered. That means we can see the other person anytime we want. Just cover your eyes, concentrate, and when you see the other one, wave, and they will wave back.*

Don: *It will be hard for the one left behind to be happy. I mean it's going to be really tough. It's going to be the hardest thing in the world because the world as we knew it has just ended.*

Ron: *When that happens, just remember what Bailey said in "The Sisterhood of the Traveling Pants:" "Maybe the truth is there's a little bit of loser in all of us, you know? Being happy isn't having everything in your life be perfect. Maybe it's about stringing together all the little things...*

... like wearing these pants...

... or getting to a new level of "Dragon's Lair"...

... and making those count for more than the bad stuff.

Maybe we just get through it...

... and that's all we can ask for."

Don: *Wow, you're right. I think that's enough said for now. We have a plan for the unthinkable. We will actually be able to see each other, and who knows, I bet we will also be able to communicate.*

Ron: *Yes.*

Letters from Don
Tiger, Tiger

"When you arrive in Hong Kong we can have a meeting with Jenny Li anytime that we want. She meets with Sir Shaw twice a week. The smartest thing we can do right now is to develop a script that they can shoot at their studio. The Bengal Tiger movie (script) you wrote would be perfect for this. Put a letter on our MCKENZIE/ASIA PRODUCTIONS stationary and get it to me."

Letters from Don
On Deal Making

"Remember when I introduced you to Jenny Li in Hong Kong at Shaw Studios where the Bruce Lee films were done? I think we are in a good position. If Jenny Li doesn't like Revenge of the Jade Lord, she will make introductions for us in Hong Kong. Maybe Revenge could be the sequel to The Protector. As far as the budget goes, Richard will tell Jenny Li that I've got the ABOVE THE LINE COSTS OUT OF Bulgaria and try and make a deal for the BELOW THE LINE COSTS from Shaw Studios. Then if he pulls that off, he goes to Bulgaria and tells them he has the BELOW THE LINE COSTS, from Shaw Studios, and he needs their ABOVE THE LINE COSTS."

Postscript

AS I PREPARE TO GO TO PRESS, I HAVE SOME UPDATES.

First, in October 2009 I traveled to New York City, to give a speech. New York was a place on our list that we wanted to visit together. Our paths had brought us to the same places several times in New York individually, but we had never been there together. So I took the trip and spent some time walking the streets of New York where I had walked alone before, and where Don had walked alone. Once, he had bought and sold diamonds in the diamond district on 47th Street and I spent time there. Ironically, the movie "The Other Guys" was in filming production and took it as a sign from Don. After I saw it in 2010, the sign was made pretty clear.

I also went to Saint Patrick's Cathedral and lit candles and said a prayer for all of my family members. This cathedral is architecture at its best. It's a space that changes your feeling. When you walk into its vastness—which is filled with light filtered by the stained glass, there is a feeling of an overpowering sense of peace. After sitting in the cathedral for a while, I walked around Rockefeller Center, and then had lunch at Trump Tower. Don and I had read all of Donald Trump's books and followed his progress in rebuilding New York. One of my most prized possessions is an autographed copy of Trump's book, **The Art of The Deal** that my wife gave to me.

Next, I walked to Central Park and found The Mall. I located the bench I had sat on when I was there many years before. It's interesting to return to a place and muse over the happenings of one's life, and the unexpected changes and twists since your last visit. After I sat there for quite a while, I strolled over to the lake where one could rent small rowboats, and then to the boat pond where electronically controlled model boats playfully fill the pond. It was a glorious day in Central Park, and I enjoyed the views of 5th

Avenue peaking through the trees and walking with the memories of my brother.

The second update to this book centers around what Don and I always did when we got to Las Vegas, which was to weigh ourselves. It's a twin thing and it was a long standing joke between us. After Don passed away I ended up seeing a chiropractor, Dr. Christy Matusiak, who helped me with a TMJ problem I was having, which was a pain and clicking problem in my jaw.

In talking with her she suggested that I make changes in my diet to improve my overall health including my cholesterol readings and other blood ratios. (I have been treated for high blood pressure and high cholesterol for over twenty-five years.) Her suggested changes were different in many ways from what the American Heart Association recommended.

Given the state of mind I was in, I decided to give it a try. On the new diet, I began eating almost thirty to forty eggs per month. Yes, that many eggs per month and I was on a low cholesterol diet! There were other key components of the diet that she taught to me and I adjusted to a new way of eating.

Long story short; in three weeks I started to lose a pound a week, and ended up losing twenty-six pounds over the next thirty weeks. At about that time I was scheduled for a cholesterol test with my cardiologist. The results showed my cholesterol went down from 155 to 133 and the two major ratios came into balance for the first time in thirty years, and other indicators were normal. Later, the cholesterol dropped to 114. I owe a huge thank you to Dr. Christy, as I call her. She has helped me in many ways, one being that I would have won the lowest weight contest with Don.

The third update is that Don's dog, Amigo, who David and Lou Anna took in and cared for, passed away in January 2010.

Don would have been so grateful that his best friends took Amigo as their own precious pet. It was reported that Amigo enjoyed two Christmas holidays with them and even wore a Santa's outfit. They visited Don's grave in Ukiah for the first time and scattered Amigo's ashes over it. Don and Amigo are now together. I can't thank David and LouAnna enough for their generosity, love and friendship.

The last update is what happened to me on a recent trip to Las Vegas. My wife and her sister were visiting their mom and took her to see the Terry Fator show. He had won the 1st place "America's Got Talent" TV show for his ventriloquism. She knew that Don and I should have been able to see that show, because tears welled up in her eyes when it began, since she was thinking of he and I. On my next trip, Pamela bought me a ticket to go.

Although I wanted to go, down inside I was filled with hesitation as I would be there alone in a crowded theater of people, and Don wouldn't be sitting next to me. It was a sell out performance and I tried to get an aisle seat so at least I wouldn't be in the middle. But of course, I couldn't get an aisle seat, so I went anyway, and ended up in the middle section, toward the back. I took my seat and waited to see who would be sitting next to mine. When the doors closed and the theater became dark, the seat next to me, was empty. The show started, and still no one sat down. It was a sold out show, and the only empty seat in the entire theater was on my left hand side where Don would have sat.

I guess Don somehow was there after all! I enjoyed the performance all the while thinking of how ironic that seat remained empty in a theater which seated over 1,200 people. I was contemplating telling the people near me at intermission, but my spooky little twin story would have probably freaked them out. It was a fabulous show. Hope he enjoyed it as much as I did!

Homage to Twinless Twins

"There is nothing better than getting a hug from a Twinless Twin."

Ron, Twin to Don

A Twinless Twin

Who am I now?
I think about you every day.
I think, I smile, I cry, I pray.
I long to have you back to stay.
To lose you was to lose myself,
I know you're in heaven, but I'm in hell.
I'm not the person I used to be.
Without my twin, how can I be?
People say they understand,
But in my heart I know they can't.
That very special bond twin's share,
they never knew it or knew my fear.
Such a heavy burden to bear,
the guilt I feel 'cause I'm still here,
Anger leading to despair.
Loneliness 'cause you're not here.
Will I ever feel whole again?
Will this grieving ever end?
And do I even want it to,
would that demean my loss of you.
I'm full of emptiness within,
Lost, Alone,
A Twinless Twin

Written by:
Mary Sweeney, twin to Joan

References
Twinless Twins Support Group International

The support group called Twinless Twins was founded and developed by Dr. Raymond W. Brandt, an identical twinless twin in 1986. It offers a strong online presence through its Web site: www.twinlesstwins.org The group also organizes a national convention each year and provides a network of regional chapter meetings where twinless twins can get together in person.

Snippets from the group's Web site. . .

Welcome to a unique support group that helps twinless twins "heal by helping" other twins.

We provide support for twins and other multiples who have lost their twin due to death or estrangement at any age. The unique aloneness we feel can best be understood by another twinless twin.

You are not alone.

Our mission is to provide a safe and compassionate community for twins to experience healing, understanding, and a desire to help others cope with the loss of their twin.

Twinless Twins Yahoo Group

This is a Yahoo-based online site where twins and others exchange information., http://health.groups.yahoo.com/group/Twinloss/

From their web site . . .Welcome to The Twin Loss Support Group for Twinless Twins. This support group is for all twins, multiple births, and parents of multiples who have lost a twin or multiple. Here, we talk, share feelings, and help each other in times of need.

We support ALL Twins and multiples that have lost their twin due to death, illness, or other types of separation. Twinless twins come here to find understanding, support and friendship from other twinless twins who understand completely how alone a twinless twin can feel.

This group should not be used for, nor is it intended to be used as a substitute for in-person, professional grief counseling and therapy. If you feel you need this type of grief counseling and therapy, please seek a professional in your area immediately. This is a non-professional, purely self-help organization: People helping other people, twins helping and sharing with other twins.

Please introduce yourself and your twin to the group if you like, and share what you want to; read everything - it helps. There are twinless twins here from every age group and every point of loss.

* * *

A good book to read that is dedicated to all Twinless Twins is called: **The Book of Twins, a Celebration in Words and Pictures** By Debra and Lisa Ganz with Alex Tresniowski, Photographs by Bill Ballenburg. Published in 1998. ISBN: 0-385-33314-5.

Some might find the stories helpful. (There are some chapters on twin loss.) My wife Pamela gave it to me shortly after Don passed away hoping it would be bring me some kind of comfort to have and read from time-to-time.

About The Author

Ronald Allen McKenzie, twin to Donald Edward McKenzie, was born on June 27, 1946 in Klamath Falls, Oregon. Ron is nine minutes and thirty-seven seconds younger than his brother Don. He resides with his wife Pamela in Illinois.

Ron became a registered architect in California in 1976 after attending Foothill Junior College in Los Altos Hills, California, and California State Polytechnic University in San Luis Obispo, California graduating in 1972 with a Bachelor in Architecture degree. He is President of COMPASS Consultants Corporation. a strategic business planning consultant, speaking at national conventions and seminars with clients coast-to-coast. He also developed Construction Peer Group Corporation, developing peer groups for CEO's and Presidents.

Ron authored Successful Business Plans for Architects with Bruce Schoumacher, which was published by McGraw Hill. He also is co-author of the Fargo Blue Mystery Series, Poolside Sting and Coyote Trap written with his brother Don. Ron continues to work on multiple writing projects including novels and screenplays to carry out concepts that he and his brother developed and discussed at great length.

You can reach me at the following internet addresses:

I can be reached via email at: rontwin2don@gmail.com

http://www.facebook.com/#!/pages/Who-Moved-The-Sun/179419175417394

OR Search for Who Moved the Sun in Facebook

http://whomovedthesun.blogspot.com

http://donmckenzie.blogspot.com

http://donmckenziephotos.blogspot.com

Obits

Two obituaries were created for Donald E. McKenzie. The first was written when filling out the initial paper work at the mortuary. The second was composed later when I returned home; it appeared in Linking Rings magazine. (A Magazine for the International Brotherhood of Magicians.)

Donald E. McKenzie

Donald E. McKenzie was born June 27, 1946, in Klamath Falls, Oregon. He passed away September 7, 2008, in Arcata, California. Resident of McKinleyville, California. Twin of Ronald A. McKenzie. Graduate of Humboldt State University with a bachelor of arts, masters in film; worked in news television as a senior editor of Entertainment Tonight, documentary films in Japan, and one of the creators of the Humboldt Film Festival. Wrote numerous screenplays and owned two bookstores on the Oregon Coast for 12 years; relocated to McKinleyville, California. Donald was co-author of the Fargo Blue Mystery Series with his twin brother Ronald.

Donald is survived by his twin brother, Ronald A. McKenzie (Pamela) of Bloomingdale, Illinois. Donald is preceded in death by his parents, father Alonzo Max and mother Janis Grace McKenzie.

Donations can be made in Donald's honor to the Seabiscuit Heritage Foundation. www.seabiscuitheritage.org

A memorial service will be held at a later date. Arrangements are under the care of Paul's Chapel 1070 H Street, Arcata, California. Please sign the guestbook at www.times-standard.com, click on obituaries.

Donald E. McKenzie

Donald E. McKenzie, 62, of McKinleyville, California, died September 7, 2008. He held I.B.M. number 27145, had been an I.B.M. member since 1974, was a member of Floating Ring 238, and member of the Order of Merlin (twenty-five years of continuous membership).

Don and his twin brother Ron got their start in magic by frequent visits to the Golden Gate Magic Company in San Francisco. They performed together for many years. Don pursued sleight of hand and supported future magicians through his donation of magic books to them. Because of his interest in magic and entertainment, Don majored in theater arts at Humboldt State University, graduating with a B.A. in Theater, followed by a Masters degree. Eventually he worked in Hollywood films, and also on the Entertainment Tonight Show, as senior video editor. Both Don and his brother made numerous trips to Las Vegas, where they met and talked with many magicians. Mr. McKenzie is survived by his twin brother Ronald.

Don's Story, His Life

Don was by all measurement an artist who first launched into photography in high school, struggled through Santa Rosa Junior College and Foothill Junior College and ended up at Humboldt State University where he majored in Theater Arts. He fell in love with Humboldt the first day he got there. He loved the Humboldt State campus, the art walk in Arcata, California, and everything that surrounded it. Through some friends he was able to get a pass to the local theaters and also landed a job at a camera store.

In the Humboldt Theater Arts Department he launched himself into film after getting a taste of it at Foothill College. He made several films with his friend David Phillips as well as others. He also directed several plays and acted in them.

He left Humboldt and ended up at KGO Television, ABC Channel 7, in San Francisco cutting news film for Van Amburg and Jerry Jensen. This was the time of the Vietnam War and he edited the Berkeley riots and tons of stories about Vietnam. When the Patty Hearst kidnapping occurred he cut all the footage that hit the national news media.

At the same time he also worked for the Archdiocesan Communication Center which created, directed and produced films and radio shows for the Catholic Church under the direction of Father Miles O' Riley and Father Harry Schlitt, who is now Monsignor Schlitt. The work there won him a San Francisco Emmy award.

Don then moved to Los Angeles and worked at several news stations such as KTLA. He was eventually picked up by Speak Up America and he cut that film for airtime. That got him noticed by

Entertainment Tonight and he started there as Senior Editor. He worked there with Dixie Whatley, Mary Hart and Leonard Maltin and others for about four years before he suffered a massive heart attack. He recuperated in Trinidad, California close to Arcata where he had attended Humboldt State University. From there he went back to Entertainment Tonight and eventually decided to move to Tokyo, Japan. First he learned broken Japanese from his tutor Saho, before making his way to Japan, where he lived and worked for over three years, picking up various assignments on documentaries and other projects.

Eventually he returned to the United States and settled in Oregon where he opened two bookstores, one in Newport and the other in Lincoln City, both of which he worked for approximately fourteen years. Then, having been forced out of his store location by an unethical landlord, and losing his life's savings from his business partner who literally stole his money and personal property and for a while, his spirit, Don moved back to McKinleyville, near Arcata, California, where he had gone to college, and melded back into his former college town and friends.

It was in Taft Lodge No. 200 A.F. & A.M., Lincoln City, Oregon where, following dad's footsteps, he became a Freemason, just as his brother did at the same time at Wheaton Lodge 269, Wheaton, Illinois. They became third degree Master Masons approximately two months apart after a year of study.

In McKinleyville, he worked with his brother on eBook projects and also had conversations with David Phillips about several movie projects. It was the good old times; he was happy and alive and feeling good about his direction.

Then it ended for him as he lost consciousness and passed away of a heart attack in the hospital emergency room on Highway 101 that he had driven past so many times in his life.

To quote Don, who wrote on August 25, 2008, just twelve days before he died, *"You always got to be ready,"* he said. *"You never know what is going to happen."*

Final Good Bye

DON AND I TEXT MESSAGED each other every day and evening. We always ended our texts in the following way. Only he and I know what it means. It's a twin thing.

Ron:
Take care of yourself. I love you

Don:
You too. I love you.

Ron:
g.a.

Don:
g.a.

* * *

The attack on America, the WTC Twin Towers, and The Twinless Twins because of it.

Do you remember how bad you felt the day the United States of America was attacked on 9-11 in 2001? No one will ever forget the images of the Twin Towers collapsing, and the bravery of all those rescuers and the firemen who went into the Twin Towers to save the people who were trapped inside.

I was in Florida getting ready to facilitate a meeting of construction executives, when, standing in the hotel lobby waiting for transportation, I saw the plane hit the tower on TV. My immediate feeling was one of overwhelming grief of all those people, and as I watched, I also thought there could be twins in the buildings.

As an architect I understood that the towers may very well fail totally, and as a twin, I was devastated to think of the loss that any surviving twin might have, as well as the sorrow for all of the inhabitants of the building. I couldn't bear the thought of what I would do if my brother ever died.

To my knowledge, up to sixteen twins have been identified being in the building, five of them identical twins. My heart goes out to them, and forever when I see an image of the Twin Towers, I think of those twins. I wanted to remember all those innocent Americans who lost their lives that day, at the Pentagon, Shanksville, PA and in particular, to those twins who died, leaving a twin behind. The Twin Towers to me is a constant reminder of my own grief.

This "Paper Dolls" Art piece was given to the author as a gift by mixed-media and fabric artist and friend of Pam, Sanna (Susan) Burgess of New Hampshire. She was inspired to make it originally as her own artistic way of remembering the attacks on America since she made them on an anniversary date. The title of it is: "Salute to The Fallen-Twins Never Forget".

Sanna's Art Blog can be found at:
www.sannasartmind.blogspot.com

Photo reprinted with permission.
©Sanna Burgess 2009.

CPSIA information can be obtained
at www.ICGtesting.com
Printed in the USA
BVHW020829200122
626302BV00009B/2